# CHENONCEAU

# chenonceau

Jean-Pierre Babelon

photographs by Jean-Pierre Godeaut

ADAM
BIRO

To Arthur et Octave
for their invaluable
technical assistance

The Menier family wishes to thank

Monsieur Bernard Voisin
for his half-century of curating the Château of Chenonceau
and Madame Nathalie Renou
for her work and devotion.

DESIGN AND LAYOUT
Louise Brody

EDITORIAL DIRECTION
Aleksandra Sokolov-Lévy

TRANSLATION FROM THE FRENCH
Michael Taylor

COPY EDITOR
Francine Brody

© 2002, Société Nouvelle Adam Biro
28, rue de Sévigné, 75004 Paris (France)

ISBN 2-87660-362-4

Printed in Italy

# contents

# A Halcyon's Nest

Picture a scarf some 150 miles long and 25 broad, winding along the banks of France's longest river. This is the hallowed territory of an outstanding body of architecture that is one of the finest treasures in humanity's heritage: the "Loire châteaux." Those two words conjure up an abundance of images, feelings, and memories. For it was here that a wonderful blend of nature and art gave society in the late fifteenth and sixteenth centuries a string of delightful, beautiful sites such as had never been matched before and would nourish many a dream in the centuries after. In their midst a new world was born, as, alongside the Valois monarchy which played such a central role in the Loire, a wealthy urban middle class, avid to show off its opulence in what had until then been exclusively a princely architecture, amassed a lion's share of the age's artistic riches. These bourgeois favored the Italian manner, the style that, having added its lace work to the old Gothic shell of the Certosa di Pavia, gradually fostered the invention of altogether new volumes and arrangements.

The Loire valley's distinctive regional identity made it an ideal setting for the French Renaissance. Its values captivated the Romantics and, indeed, all succeeding generations. Balzac, who was born in Tours, brought tears to the eyes of his readers when the hero of his novel *Le Lys dans la Vallée* speaks the following words to the woman he loves: "Do not ask me again why I love the Touraine. I do not love it as one loves one's birthplace or a desert oasis; I love it as an artist loves art; I love it less than I love you, but were it not for the Touraine I might no longer be alive." Turning to his beloved landscape, he sweeps on, "One comes on a valley there beginning at Montbazon and ending at the Loire, which seems to frisk below the castles poised on those twin rows of hills; a magnificent emerald bowl at the bottom of which the Indre coils with the motions of a snake."[1]

The white castles of the Loire require a garden setting blessed with a climate of proverbial mildness. They require the proximity of forests sheltering the supreme pleasures of hunting. Were they not offset by water flowing nearby, they would seem less dazzling—and no rivers better serve this purpose than the Loire and its tributaries. Of all the gemlike châteaux spangling their valleys is there one that could possibly rival Chenonceau? Was there ever a palace the river gods and aquatic nymphs loved more and lavished as many gifts on? Chenonceau is not just perched on the banks of the Cher; it stands squarely in mid-stream and the fleeting reflections of the river play over its pale façades. It was made for watery landscapes to be brought

10

[1] See J.-P. Babelon, "Les châteaux de la Loire," in Pierre Nora (ed.), *Les lieux de la mémoire,* Part III, vol. 3, Paris, Gallimard, 1992, pp. 402-449.

into its bed-chambers, its galleries, even its staircase, as if to assuage some irrepressible obsession with fluidity.

For centuries its spell has been unbroken. Almost from the outset the small castle's exquisite beauty caught the eye of King Francis I who, on mounting the throne, managed to wrest it from his treasurer, who had built it. Then Francis's successor, Henry II, gave it to his mistress Diane de Poitiers. After Henry's death, his mother Catherine de' Medici spared no effort to get it back from the former favorite. The magic of Chenonceau's water-girt architecture inspired the two women—Diane and Catherine—to build a bridge and galleries over the Cher behind the original castle erected by Thomas and Catherine Bohier, not caring much whether the scale of the new construction accorded with the refined proportions of the earlier structure. The château's successive owners, most of them women, all cherished it, showing perhaps that the castle and its grounds, so fortunately spared by the vicissitudes of history, have always embodied an ideal of what a home should be. As the thousands and thousands of visitors who flock to it from all over the world unfailingly observe, there has never been anything quite like Chenonceau before or after.

Once the day's last tourist has gone, under the beams of Diana's crescent moon the Bohiers' manor-house reverts to its solitude in the lap of the river. It seems to float there like a nest of halcyons, those fabled birds once credited with the power to lull storms when raising their young.

11

# 1
## A château born on water

## The Origins

The late nineteenth-century historian Léon Palustre advised visitors to approach Chenonceau from the river. At the time steam launches still sailed up the Cher from Tours, and boats could be had for hire in nearby Bléré. The château can still be reached by water and this remains the most poetic way of discovering its magnificent site with its forest-shaded currents. When the long, magical silhouette of the aqueduct-like castle is revealed in the brightness of dawn or the fiery glow of evening, the visual impact it makes is indescribable.

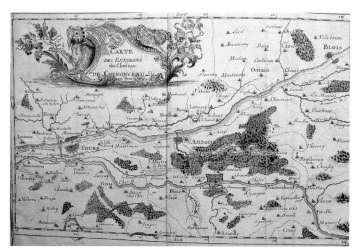

∧ Chenonceau and surroundings. Hand-drawn and watercolored map by Dupas de La Chauvinière, 1735 (CHENONCEAU ARCHIVES, VOL.107). The old spelling *Chenonceau* is still used for the château, while the eighteenth-century *Chenonceaux* designates the neighboring village.

Approaching more prosaically by land, you follow an avenue lined with plane trees southward for a little over half a mile along the axis that dictated the layout of the château and its grounds. To the north, an eight-mile road between the Cher and the Loire cuts across the forest to Amboise, the seat of the barony Chenonceau formerly belonged to. That stronghold was held by the Amboise family until 1434, when the king of France confiscated it from Louis d'Amboise, who had been found guilty of felony, and built what was to become one of the royal family's favorite residences. The geographic, feudal, and affective ties between Chenonceau and Amboise are a permanent feature of the history of the two châteaux and their successive owners have kept up a privileged connection with each other. The masters of Amboise have been inclined to view Chenonceau as a delightful annex of the royal fortress, while the proprietors of Chenonceau have always sent to Amboise, if not to Tours, for masons and other craftsmen.

Chenonceau is situated on the road that runs along the right bank of the Cher between Montrichard and Tours. There is no fortified escarpment here commanding the river and controlling a strategically-important bridge, as is the case with the region's most well-known châteaux, Blois and Amboise on the Loire, Loches on the Indre, Chinon on the Vienne, all of them confiscated by the throne when the Touraine became the heart of the kingdom and Tours its capital, basically between 1440 and 1520. The reason no bridge spans the Cher at Chenonceau, almost 100 yards across at this point,[2] is paradoxical: the château itself was turned into a kind of private bridge. Nevertheless, for the lords of Chenonceau it was vital to control the busy line of communications and traffic in timber and building materials, salt, wine, and fodder along the river Cher between the Sologne and the Berry on the one hand and, on the other, the Touraine, the Anjou, and the sea port of Nantes and its surrounding country. For obvious reasons, they wanted their sovereignty to extend over both banks of the river.

On the left bank the terrain consists of meadows irrigated by a stream, the Vestin, which slopes down gently from a line of hills enclosing the site to the south. The château des Houdes, erected on the territory of Francueil, was a necessary adjunct to Chenonceau's defense. On this bank, along which ran the Roman road linking Tours to Lyon, vestiges of a Roman villa have been found. Obviously the beauty of the site had appealed to some prosperous Gallo-Roman

[2] J. Guillaume (1969) established that the "wooden or stone" bridge mentioned in King Francis I's letter of patent of December 1517 has nothing to do with the château of Chenonceau, but a public bridge that may have stood upstream at Chisseaux on the road to Franceuil. Only in the nineteenth century was the latter erected to serve as a crossing for the D 80 road.

17

landowner. Opposite, on the right bank, between Civray and Chisseaux, where traces of other Roman dwellings were discovered, the village of Chenonceau sprang up in the eleventh century, judging from the style of its church's apse. It is referred to as the *parochia de Chenoncello* in documents from the twelfth century on, as the abbé Chevalier, to whom we owe most of our knowledge of Chenonceau, established in the nineteenth century.[3]

## The Marques' Castle

We know that in the thirteenth century a castle stood on the right bank of the Cher. It belonged to the Marques family, ordinary knights from the Auvergne or the Marche who answered to the name of Guillaume or Robert. This stronghold's key position for controlling the Cher and protecting the city of Tours, which remained loyal to the Valois kings, was such that it was fought over and damaged several times in the course of the Hundred Years' War. When hostilities flared up again in 1555 and Edward III of England landed in Calais, his son, the Black Prince, marched north from Guyenne to the Loire, laying waste the Berri, the Sologne, the valleys of the Cher and Indre. By order of the Governor of Tours, loyal to King John the Good, his forces' camps at Azay-sur-Cher and Cormery were burned down.

After the French defeat at Poitiers, the treaty of Brétigny in 1360 failed to establish peace and left marauding troops free to plunder and set fire to everything on their path. Two knights, Olivier and Bertrand du Guesclin, nephews of the future *connétable* of Charles V, succeeded in driving out the looters from the castles of Montlouis, Les Houdes, and Chenonceau. In the reign of Charles VI, Jean Marques made the mistake of siding against the Dauphin and opening his fortresses to the English. Despatched to the Touraine to oppose the latter, Maréchal Boucicaut defeated them in 1411 in the meadows of

[3] The history of Chenonceau is exceptionally well documented. Despite the loss of several royal titles burnt by revolutionaries in 1793, a veritable treasure trove of "royal archives" containing 4250 separate documents in 137 bound volumes is still preserved at the château. It is these archives that enabled the abbé and, later, prelate Casimir Chevalier to write his detailed history of the château. The parish priest of Civray-sur-Cher at the time, the abbé was invited in 1859 by the Comte de Villeneuve to classify the documents in the castle and to publish a portion of them. In 1868, the abbé wrote confidently, "As far as concerns Chenonceau, few things remain to be explored after us."

the Vestin on the Cher's south bank. He then burned down and razed the castles
of the treacherous vassal, both at Chenonceau and at Les Houdes (where traces
of this destruction could still be seen in the nineteenth century)[4] and gave
orders that the timber on both estates be cut down to "infamy's level."

The felon's son, Jean II Marques, strove to regain the family's lost honor.
He paid off his father's debts and petitioned Charles VII for permission to rebuild
the castle of his forebears. Once the reconquest of France got underway with
the help of Joan of Arc the king wished to strengthen his power in the Touraine,
where Tours, Amboise, Loches and Chinon were his only strongholds. So in his
letter patent of 1432 he gave his sanction to Jean II Marques' request. The latter
chose a new site to build his castle on, right on the edge of the Cher, to take
advantage of the natural protection the river offered. He drew a rough square
on the bank (164 x 180 feet) and had it terraced and reinforced with masonry
to make a raised platform surrounded on three sides by a moat of flowing water
connected to the river. To the north, a fortified farmyard, probably built
on the ruins of the former manor, defended the new castle's drawbridge.

After the fashion of many strongholds of this time, like Plessis-Bourré, built for
King Louis XI's favorite, Jean Bourré, from 1468 on, Jean II Marques' château
most likely consisted of four round corner towers surrounded by a moat and
connected either by curtain walls or by a central building flanking a massive
fortified gate. Today all that remains of this structure is the *grosse tour,*
the south-west tower, the largest of the four and the seigniory's symbolic seat.
Traces of construction on one of its sides suggest that another construction
originally abutted it to the north. Behind it, directly on the river to be able to
use the driving force of the current, Marques had a mill erected on two massive

All subsequent studies
are based on the dozen
or so works he published,
chiefly between 1860 and
1870, with the approval
of the Academy of
Poitiers and the Academie
des Inscriptions et Belles-
Lettres in Paris. The abbé
Chevalier was typical
of the great nineteenth-
century ecclesiastical
scholars who deserve
the gratitude of later
generations for having
written much of France's
regional history. As
president of the Société
archéologique de Touraine
and permanent secretary
of the Société
d'Agriculture, Science,
Arts et Belles-Lettres
of the Indre-et-Loire,
he was interested in
geology, hydrography and
agriculture, and nothing
concerning the Touraine
escaped his ken.
[4] C. Chevalier, *Histoire de
Chenonceau,* 1868, p. 62.

19

∧ The fifteenth-century quadrangular castle of Le Plessis-Bourré at Ecuillé, Maine-et-Loire (Archives photographiques des Monuments historiques).

5 The slits one sees on the north side of the first pier are probably contemporary with the work undertaken for the Bohiers: they resemble the openings made for Gilles Berthelot at Azay-le-Rideau.

stone piers. This enabled him to levy a tax on the local peasants who were obliged to mill their harvests at the castle. The mill may also have served a defensive purpose.[5]

The cost of the construction depleted the Marques' finances and hastened the decline of the family's next generation. Though married to Martine Bérart, the daughter of a royal treasurer and steward to Louis XI, Pierre Marques was a spendthrift. To increase his domain at Chenonceau, he made reckless acquisitions, ran up debts, and had to mortgage his properties. He was left with no option in the end but to put his seigniories up for sale one by one, notably Les Houdes. Learning of this, a wealthy, recently ennobled bourgeois of Tours, the *général de finances* Thomas Bohier, moved to acquire Chenonceau. Acting secretly, he had agents gradually buy up Pierre Marques and his wife's annuities and estates. In 1494 he was able to get hold of Les Houdes. Only once he had judged that the latter were reduced to selling Chenonceau did he reveal his true identity. Dated June 3, 1496, the deed of sale sets the price at 7374 *livres tournois* and 10 *sols*.

Bohier thought he had attained his goal but had not reckoned on the chicanery of feudal law. Like every one of Chenonceau's purchasers in the centuries to come, he was obliged to summon lawyers and endless reserves of patience to get his way. The first obstacle he encountered was that the Marques moved to farm the lands at Chenonceau on lease. They hung on for a while but soon, unable to pay even the first term, had no choice but to leave the estate and retire to the manor of Le Couldray at Saint-Martin-le-Beau. Then, in 1499, one of Pierre Marques' brothers, Guillaume, invoked the clause of lineal annulment which allowed any family member of a seller of noble property (up to ten times removed) to buy back his inheritance at the selling price.

But Guillaume Marques died in the middle of these legal proceedings, before he had gathered the funds needed to pay off the Bohiers. His daughter Catherine continued his efforts and moved into Chenonceau, in full view of the small turreted manor that Thomas Bohier had rebuilt at Les Houdes. Soon after, she married François Fumée, lord of Les Fourneaux and a son of Louis XI's powerful chief physician and keeper of the seals. Then she boldly asserted her sovereignty over Les Houdes, obliging Bohier to pay homage to her. The legal battle raged on for another nine years and ended with the confiscation of Chenonceau and its sale by auction before the bailiff's court of Tours on February 8, 1513, for the sum of 15,641 *livres*. Forced to leave, Catherine and her husband spent the rest of their days living at Les Fourneaux. Thomas Bohier, relishing victory after sixteen years of continuous litigation, formally took possession of Chenonceau on February 10. He then hastened to pay homage to King Louis XII's representative, Étienne Poncher, Bishop of Paris, during a ceremony that took place on February 17 at the château of Blois.

23

∧ The manor of Les Houdes (or Les Oudes or Les Ouldes) at Franceuil. Watercolored drawing by Dupas de La Chauvinière, 1735 (CHENONCEAU ARCHIVES, VOL. 107).

# 2

## THE BOHIERS' CHÂTEAU

*The location, place and castle of Chenonceau*
*[...] is a comely site and house standing*
*upon the river Cher in fair and pleasing country*
*hard by our forests of Amboise and*
*Montrichard where we are wont to hunt and*
*sport, and we may sometimes lodge at the*
*said castle and house of Chenonceau.*

King Francis I, letter patent of December 1517

## Thomas Bohier

Thomas Bohier was a perfect representative of the wealthy merchant class of Tours in whose midst King Louis XI, placing his trust in men skilled in commerce and business, recruited his counselors and financiers, elevating them to positions of importance as a counterweight to the arrogant aristocracy always too inclined to switch sides. A number of families linked by marriage formed a sort of trust from whose ranks a score of individuals gained a virtual monopoly over the management, if not control, of royal revenues and expenditures. In the Church too some of them found opportunities for careers of the greatest brilliance. The Bohiers and the Briçonnets, the Beaune-Semblançays, the Berthelots, as well as the Duprats and the Ponchers, formed a remarkable pool of talent. Rich and clever men, they were art lovers too, and undertook to build town mansions and country manors in a style that trumpeted their recent rise in status. In doing so they quickened, sometimes even before the king himself, the flowering of the new Renaissance architecture in the Loire— Guillaume Briçonnet and his son Jean at Plessis-Rideau (les Réaux), Denis Briçonnet at the priory of Coussay-en-Mirebalais, Gilles Berthelot at Azay-le-Rideau.

They enjoyed the favor of the French kings until the tide turned after the battle of Pavia where Francis I was made prisoner, leaving his mother, the cool-headed Louise of Savoy, to govern as she pleased. Angered at the staggering cost of the Italian wars, the regent, who also bore a number of personal grudges against the men who held the kingdom's purse strings, goaded the king as soon as he returned from captivity to set up a committee to investigate their dealings. Thus it was that in the terrible winter of 1527 the 82 year-old *surintendant* Semblançay was hung at Montfaucon, despite his years, before the incredulous stares of the citizens of Paris.

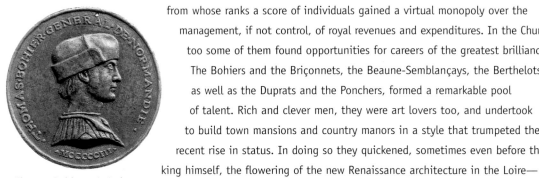

∧ Thomas Bohier, *général des finances* of Normandy. Token struck in 1503 (Bibliothèque national de France, cabinet des médailles).

28

Thomas Bohier was, like the Marques, of Auvergnat stock. He was born
at Issoire in the second half of the sixteenth century into a family
of respectable merchants. His father Austremoine had married Béraude du Prat,
the aunt of Antoine Duprat, Francis I's chancellor in 1515, later Archbishop
of Sens, who had become a cardinal in 1527 and had built the castle of
Nantouillet in the Brie. Moreover, thanks to his marriage to Catherine Briçonnet,
Thomas Bohier entered a family firmly established in the royal entourage.
Catherine's father, Guillaume Briçonnet, the son of Tour's first mayor and
a Bertholet daughter, had made a brilliant dual career. Having married
Raoulette de Beaune, the sister of the unfortunate Semblençay, he was
successively *général des finances* in Languedoc and *surintendant*. Then,
after his wife died, he entered a religious order and, thanks to Charles VIII,
whose favorite he became—he was one of the principal instigators of the
Naples expedition—rose to high ecclesiastical positions. He was successively
bishop of Saint-Malo and Nîmes, cardinal, archbishop of Rheims and
Narbonne. Two of his sons, Denis and Guillaume, were bishops. As abbot
of Saint-Germain-des-Près and bishop of Meaux, the latter introduced Erasmus's
new exegesis of the Holy Scriptures into France and was thus instrumental
in furthering the Reformation there.

Thomas Bohier, for his part, had early on entered the royal administration.
Appointed notary and royal secretary in 1491, a position that carried a title
of nobility, he became chamberlain to Charles VIII, master of accounts
of the city of Paris, and *général des finances* of Normandy. As such he had
the power to levy taxes, if need be by force, and to allocate public
expenditures, though with the obligation to make up for any shortfalls
out of his own personal fortune, reimbursing himself later if and when feasible.

< The Bohiers' château seen from
the top of the Marques' Tower.

∧ The château from the entrance avenue.

His responsibilities as a financial administrator led him to take an active part in the French royalty's Italian expeditions, with twofold consequences.

On the one hand, his frequent, prolonged absences meant that his wife Catherine Briçonnet became personally involved in the construction of the new castle at Chenonceau. She kept close watch on the progress of the work and was the first of the "ladies of Chenonceau" so passionately occupied in the centuries to come in building and embellishing the château and its gardens. On the other hand, Thomas Bohier's sojourns south of the Alps made him particularly receptive to architectural innovations in the Duchy of Milan and, more generally, throughout the Italian peninsula. Bohier first saw Italy with Charles VIII in 1494; he accompanied Louis XII; in 1507 he took part in the expedition against Genoa, where he was knighted by Charles of Amboise. In 1511, he was appointed secretary of finances in Italy. The year 1512 saw him in Milan. Back in France early in 1513, he returned to Milan in May, then again in 1514 and 1515 in the retinue of Francis I, who raised him to even more absorbing and important responsibilities as chief administrator of the Duchy of Milan. Bohier returned to Italy in 1521, with the Count of Lautrec, as paymaster general and even, after the French defeat at La Bicoque, as lieutenant-general. And it was in Italy that he died, at the camp of Vigelli in the territory of Milan, on March 24, 1524.

### Building the Château

For Thomas Bohier, who was the mayor of Tours and already owned one of the finest houses in the city, formerly on the rue de la Scellerie, the construction of the new castle at Chenonceau was to be a dazzling expression of the eminent position he had attained and a proclamation of the fact that he henceforth belonged to the kingdom's aristocracy. Thus, before the work even commenced, he set his mind on giving the domain he had so patiently amassed and constantly

[6] After erecting his castle on the mill's piles, Bohier established another mill on boats a short distance downstream. The mill was later destroyed and its public charge was transferred to the moulin-fort built on the Cher in 1545 opposite Chisseaux. Some three centuries later this fortified mill was destroyed to make way for the Canal du Berry.

sought to expand a more elevated rank in the feudal hierarchy. He petitioned to have the six fiefs he had acquired joined together into a single castellany encompassing 1680 hectares scattered over some ten parishes. King Louis XII gave his consent and by February 1514 Thomas Bohier was able to exercise his rights as lord of the manor. These included a number of honorific prerogatives, the authority to render justice on his own lands, and the economic benefits of a substantial revenue from hunting and fishing, tolls, markets and seasonal fairs, the public water mill[6] and certain tithes. In return he owed his suzerain the king, lord of the barony at Amboise on which Chenonceau was dependent, fealty and armed personal service in the event of an enemy invasion.[7] Louis XII having died prematurely after his marriage to Henry VIII of England's sister, Mary Tudor —a marriage Bohier had gone to England to negotiate in June 1514—he made homage to Francis I at the latter's coronation on February 27, 1515.

Surviving records of expenses allow one to follow the building of the château. They make it clear that the castle's plan was established as early as Thomas Bohier's sojourn in Touraine during the first months of 1513, before he left for Milan. Instead of embellishing the quadrangular fortress built in 1432, which would have been the ordinary course of action for the time, Bohier decided to have it razed and to use the moat-surrounded platform on which it had stood as the access to a new castle. This was a capital decision. The estate's entire composition was thus determined by a north-south axis. The castle was to be approached down a straight avenue leading to a gate flanked by two towers joined to the farm buildings of La Grange.[8] Skewing to the left, a second avenue was to run past a group of service buildings and gardens known as "le Pavillon" (or the "Pavillon de Marques") connected to the old castle's farmyard. This was to lead to the drawbridge and, from there, slanting rightward across the terrace, to the edge of the Cher.

[7] In 1515 Bohier built in the village of Chenonceau the castellany's "palace" or audience hall for rendering local justice as well as a covered market, which was later remodeled into a page's house and still has an interesting stairway. He also had the nave of the parish church rebuilt. It was consecrated in 1515 by Thomas Bohier's brother-in-law Denis Briçonnet, Bishop of Saint-Malo.

[8] This lay-out is visible on Du Cerceau's general plan and bird's eye view of Chenonceau, circa 1560, reproduced on p. 109. One can clearly distinguish the original avenue from Diane de Poitier's axial approach. Close to the tenant farm, a circular structure now housing a water reservoir may be a remnant of the fortified gate.

∧ The moat skirting Diane's parterre
on the north side.

> The moat behind the Pavillon de la Chancellerie
looking toward the north.

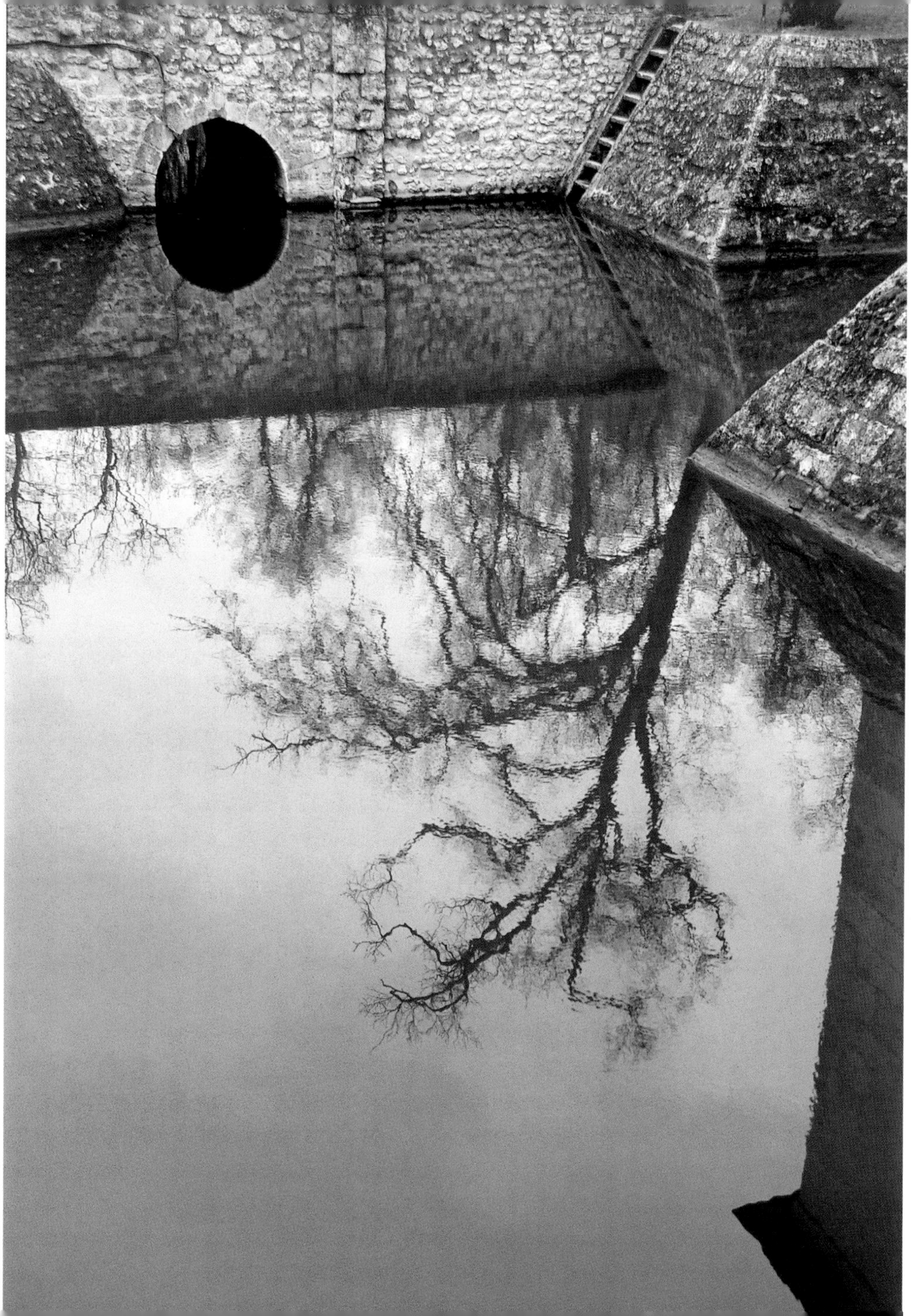

∧ The well on the Marques' terrace and the steps to the tower entrance.

∧ The Marques' Tower, east view.

In a bold departure from tradition, the new castle was to perch on the water mill's piles. The openings of its north façade were to be designed in relation to the main approach. Strictly axial compositions of this nature were just beginning to appear in France at this time—in the design of the Maréchal de Gié's estate in the Anjou, Le Verger, laid out after the latter's return from Italy in 1498, and, a little later, in the castle of Bury near Blois, built in 1514 for the secretary of state Florimond Robertet.[9]

[9] Unfortunately, only vestiges of these two buildings survive.

The old Marques' fortress, however, having been the foundation of the new *châtellenie* of Chenonceau and the emblem of the feudal continuity associated with the noble site, had to be left standing. Similarly, the bulky dungeon which

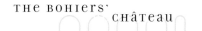

[10] Léon Palustre and, later, François Gébelin (1927, p. 81) believed that the tower's sculpted décor, which is superior to that of the château, was the work of a first team of stone carvers active at Chenonceau as early as 1513. Jean Guillaume (2001, p. 40), on the other hand, thinks that it was executed later by the stone carvers who worked on the lower gallery and were influenced by the Francis I wing at Blois.

[11] Dated January 29, 1522, this document commissions an anonymous craftsman from Tours to tile and "daub" (with a mixture of thatch and mud) the partitions of the attic gallery and garret rooms, and to finish with a "whitewash of brick hue" like one he had executed at Veretz, "and if possible better." (Chenonceau archives, 5/19, published in *Bulletin de la société archéologique de Touraine,* vol. II, and in *Nouvelles archives de l'art français,* 1872, pp. 151-153). Located near Montlouis-sur-Loire, the castle of Véretz was built for Jean de La Barrre, a former chamberlain of King Charles VIII. Its construction had started in 1519.

was the main seat of all the kingdom's fiefs had long stood in the middle of the royal Louvre, and only in 1528 had King Francis I dared to have it torn down. So Thomas Bohier decided to leave one element of the original castle, the Tower of the Marques, on the platform before the new castle, as a memorial to the domain's previous lords. But though the two-headed eagle of the Marques' coat-of-arms still adorns the coping of the neighboring well, Bohier had the initials TBK—for Thomas Bohier and Catherine Briçonnet—carved on the tower.

After having it remodeled, the Bohiers probably moved into this large tower while the old castle was being demolished, or so it would seem from the date 1513 on the campanile bell. The work on the tower was undertaken to give it a less forbidding top, one more in keeping with the Loire style: a covered way resting on small corbels in lieu of machicolations, a high conic roof, doors, windows, and dormer frames carved in white stone set into the existing masonry coated with mortar, where one can still make out traces of the old fortress's loopholes.[10] The doors to the tower and that of the elegant stairwell turret abutting it are enhanced by the exquisitely architectural stone steps leading up to them, recalling the perrons at Bury, Nantouillet, and the first Chantilly. They contribute to the tower's impressive *mise en scène*.

Work on the castle on the river got underway in 1514 or 1515 during one of Thomas Bohier's prolonged residences in the Touraine. Judging from the description of the castle in Francis I's letter patent of December of that year and the fact that the chapel was consecrated in 1518 by Bohier's brother, Cardinal Antoine, Archbishop of Bourges, the main structure was completed by the end of 1517. The château's decoration carried on until 1521, the date inscribed on the chapel gallery and recorded in a 1522 contract for last-minute work.[11] The description

∧ The decorated chimneys,
   south side.

> The chapel apse. The bell turret and the statue
  of the Virgin date from Madame Pelouze's restoration.

[12] Abbé Casimir Chevalier, *Archives royales de Chenonceau*, vol. I, 1864, p. 70.

[13] *Voyage en France du sieur Du Buisson*, a gentleman serving Monsieur de Guénégaud. Manuscript 2694 in the Bibliothèque Mazarine in Paris, analyzed by Prince Augustin Galitzin in *Mémoires de la Société Archéologique de Touraine*, vol. XI, 1859, pp. 130-136, and published in C. Chevalier, *Archives royales*, vol. I, 1864, pp. XXVII-XXXI.

[14] An elegant stone quarried above Montrichard and used as well in the construction of the châteaux of Chaumont, Blois, and Chambord.

[15] Léon Palustre believed that these piles were reinforced to bear the weight of the castle. The quality of the stonework and the openings that were made suggest that this may well have been the case.

accompanying Thomas Bohier's statement of the castellany's holdings in 1523[12] is perfectly clear: "My castle and stronghold of Chenonceau, which I have caused to be rebuilt, constructed, and erected upon the river Cher, which flows on every side of my aforesaid castle, and the tower of the aforesaid place which I have had reconstructed and repaired," and, further on, "my mill which formerly belonged to the aforementioned Chenonceau, resting on the two pillars upon which my castle now stands, which mill I have caused to be pulled down and dismantled..."

Built on an almost perfect square plan of 22 by 23 meters (68 by 71 feet) not counting walls and turrets, the castle broke with all the practices of the time and was long to be a source of wonder to visitors. "From the bridge you enter into a courtless hall," writes a passing traveler in 1659[13]... "This hall is in fact a passing strange pavilion, possessing no architectural order, adorned with atlantes and caryatids fashioned any old way; it is square, built of white Bourray stone,[14] has a slate roof..." How could a castle function without an inner court? The court's role was in fact filled by two alternative elements: the terrace of the Marques on the outside, where the presence of the tower visually connected the open space with the château, and, inside, the central vestibule creating a convenient passage from one part of the building to the other.

The former mill's infrastructure, the two massive piers[15] resting on the river's rocky bed and the elongated arch that had housed its wheel, provided a base for the new structure. It determined the rectangular platform whose surface is mostly occupied by the square castle, some thirty feet above the river.[16] The combined roofs of the main building immediately reveal the castle's structure. To the east and west one sees two oblong *corps de logis* each crowned with a straight peaked roof, and between them, the central north-south-oriented

∧ The stone carving above the tower door. A fifteenth-century Virgin acquired by Madame Pelouze stands in the niche.

∧ The door of the Bohiers' château flanked by projecting half-moon balconies.

[16] The ground floor apartments are normally 32 to 33 feet above the water and the Cher never floods higher than twenty feet above its customary level, or so we learn from the *Discours historique sur la châtellenie et le château de Chenonceau* written in 1745 by Dupas de La Chauvinière (published in A. Galitzin, *Mémoires de la Société archéologique de Touraine*, vol. IX, 1857, pp. 102-144.

volume containing the vestibule and the first-floor gallery is capped by a third roof, abutting the first two and perpendicular to them, effectively closing the box-like structure. The roofs' height is determined by their sixteenth-century framework which was in turn dependent on the length of the timbers at the roofers' disposal. Tall chimneys adorned with vertical ribs creating the illusion of niches topped with seashells bring variety and life to these roofs.

Ignoring the adventitious constructions on the east façade of Bohier's castle and on the south façade of the gallery bridge, one is inevitably struck by the rigorousness of the central block's design. Each of the four façades is divided

regularly into three bays, each containing one transom window per floor, framed
by pilasters and crowned with a tall dormer. The central bays are emphasized by
their extra width, the fact that they project outward, and by the dormer's added
height and more elaborate crowning structure. The cornice consists of a tall
frieze of semicircular balusters recalling those of the interior stairway, a motif
which may have inspired the balustrade topping the façade at Chambord.
Below it, twin courses of continuous moldings intersect the bays' vertical lines,
but with none of the extreme regularity to be seen at Blois or Chambord.
The master of Chenonceau does not seem to have insisted on a systematic grid,
for his builders interrupted the façade lines by inserting between the ground-
floor and first-floor openings broad tables upon which rich circular medallions
were to be placed (only on the north façade were these decorations completed).

43

Tall cylindrical turrets rise at the four corners. One sees similar ones, built from
the ground level up, at the old royal residence of Loches and at Francis I's *logis*
in Amboise. They are a standard rhythmical feature of earlier architecture, but at
Chenonceau they become true bartizans and the squinches on which they stand are
lavishly decorated with horizontal moldings. This was to become a characteristic
feature of Loire architecture, notably at Azay-le-Rideau. Overhanging elements
in the Flamboyant tradition are conspicuous at Chenonceau, and this is not simply
due to the whims of its conceivers: the technique of projecting structures from
walls made it possible for balconies to be placed wherever the pleasure of viewing
the landscape called for them. Thus semicircular balconies billow out from the
entrance façade on either side of the door (as they do at the ducal palace in Nancy)
in a pattern repeated on the level of the parapets of the forecourt and bridge
leading to the château. A basket-handle-shaped loggia provided with a balcony,
its oblong salience framed by two cut-off corners, such as one sees at Ainay-le-Vieil

<
The château's
north façade,
its regular,
symmetrical
design contrasting
with the lines
of the chapel
on the left.

and on Blois' Louis XII façade, juts out from the center of the west face and, before the construction of the gallery bridge, an identical one graced the south side.[17]

∧ The chapel and the Bohiers' library perched above the piers of the old Marques' mill.

The reconstruction of the latter façade based on surviving elements[18] shows us that to the left of the bay closing off the inner gallery and the balcony above the Cher, the construction of a straight stairway leading down to the kitchens built inside the piers below the ground-floor apartments required the builders to widen the outer wall by designing an overhanging mass of masonry on the ground floor. This meant substituting a bay of half-width windows for the regular full-window bay, a breach of symmetry visible only from the river's south bank.

[17] Such projections with cut-off corners were unusual at this time. Examples exist from a later date at Ecouen and at Francis I's castle at Cognac. Nantouillet, too, displays a corbelled mass of stonework on its later façade.
[18] Using architect Felix Roguet's 1865 drawing in the château archives, Jean Guillaume produced this reconstruction in 1969.

Well aware that a perfectly symmetrical building viewed freely as an architectural object on water would eventually prove to be monotonous, Thomas Bohier chose to borrow from the old Gothic spirit various adventitious elements as felicitous departures from the monotony of an excessively regular plan. On the east side there remained unoccupied space on the mill's rectangular platform. Above the pointed tips of the piers designed to break the Cher's current and deflect it toward the mill wheel two small structures were erected and connected by a terrace. The lacy outlines of these twin structures conceived as excrescences on the façade looking toward the rising sun stand out sharply with their stairwell turrets against the sober regularity of the castle's design. To one side lies the chapel; to the other, the small edifice connected on the ground floor and first floor to the apartments of the master of Chenonceau and his wife. It was here, on the lower level of the *logis*, that Thomas Bohier installed his *studiolo,* his private study and library.

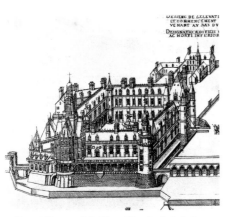

DESIGN DE L'ELEVATI ET COMMENCEMENT VENANT AY BAS DV DESIGNATIO AEDIFICI AC HORTI INFERIOR

∧ The château of Gaillon (Eure). Detail from a plate in Jacques Androuet Du Cerceau's *Les Plus Excellents Bastiments de France* (vol. I, 1576) showing the chapel and the tower housing the apartments of Cardinal d'Amboise.

Precedents for this singular arrangement have naturally been looked for. There is the chapel of St Hubert audaciously poised on the rampart at Amboise, and there is Gaillon where the elaborate silhouettes of the chapel and the tower housing the apartments of Cardinal Georges d'Amboise rose on either side of a terrace overlooking the Seine valley.[19] If one recalls as well that the logis at the rear of this terrace was crowned with a frieze of demi-balusters, it seems obvious that either the construction of Gaillon influenced that of Chenonceau or that the same teams worked on both edifices, for, in spite of the difference in scale, the resemblance between them are too numerous to be accidental. The great castle of Gaillon,

45

[19] Jean Guillaume established the unquestionable parallel with Gaillon. Although no longer discernible today, given Gaillon's present state, this arrangement is quite visible on Du Cerceau's engraving and on a drawing in the Cronstedt Collection in Stockholm.

the seat of the archbishops of Rouen, was built for an opulent *tourangeau,* Cardinal Georges d'Amboise, Louis XII's powerful minister and another enthusiastic advocate of the French expeditions to Italy. He was appointed Viceroy of the Duchy of Milan in 1500 and even entertained hopes of wearing the pontifical tiara. On his return to France he began to remodel Gaillon, at first in the Gothic spirit with master-builders from Tours (1502-1506), then with masons and stone carvers from Rouen more open to Italian influences (1506-1510). Having met in Milan on numerous occasions, he and Thomas Bohier were well acquainted with each other. Moreover, Bohier was the *général des finances* in Normandy where Gaillon was located.

### An Original Plan

If the conception and sculpted décor of Chenonceau's façades looked back to the sixteenth-century's early masterpieces—especially the characteristic transformation of the tall central dormers with their flamboyant moldings into elaborate structures ornamented with pilasters, pinnacles, and pediments—the château's plan is distinguished by its utter originality and its harmonious fusion of modular regularity and convenience. It is the creation of an independent and innovative mind and reflects the choices of the master of the house or perhaps his wife. A long vaulted gallery-like vestibule 12 feet broad and 68 feet long (3.90 x 22 m.), traverses the building from front to back, and provides direct access to the apartments. The rooms of the latter are twice as wide as the central hall: two bed-chambers to the right and, to the left, a chamber and a *salle des gardes*. Entered from the main door beneath its inscription honoring King Francis I and Queen Claude of France, the vestibule runs straight to a large bay window and balcony in the middle of the south façade overlooking the Cher. The same arrangement, minus vaults, is repeated on the first floor and in the attic. A wardrobe and privy in each of the four corner turrets provided an added measure of comfort for each room.

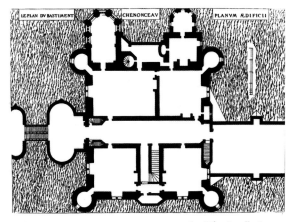

∧ Plan of the château in Du Cerceau's *Les Plus Excellents Bastiments de France* (vol. II, 1579), with the entrance on the left and the projected gallery on the right.

48

This innovation is combined with a second novelty: the position and layout of the staircase on the right, half-way down the vestibule. It is not the spiral type,

∧ Second flight of the main stairs above
  the midway turn.

∧ The midway turn and the bays providing
  it with light.

20 The flights between the
first and second floors
were built and decorated
in 1869-1870 by Roguet.

thoroughly traditional in French building at the time and destined to remain
in fashion for a long time to come. Its straight flights are organized ramp to ramp,
a system that was then making its appearance at the châteaux of Josselin
and Bury. Having opted for this solution favored by Italian builders, Chenonceau's
master took stunning liberties with it, for instead of pausing at an intermediate
landing which serves as the departure for the upper flight in reverse direction,
the stairway twists in a 180-degree turn. Between the stairs and the castle's outer
wall on the west a space about three feet (1 m.) wide is left open from ground
to attic through a clever arrangement of buttressed arches—another remarkable
invention.[20] The exceptional breadth and height of the west façade's central window
floods the stairs with natural light and one is greeted with a view of the Cher's

[21] The two loggia stairways at the Château of Châteaudun, successive stages in resolving the problem of how to let natural light into a staircase, prefigure the Chenonceau system, which in turn influenced the stairs at Azay-le-Rideau.

[22] Except, we believe, the "new" castle at Bourdeilles erected shortly after 1589 by Jacquette de Montbron, who had admired Chenonceau's well-lit central corridor and the fine views it commanded when accompanying Catherine de' Medici and Louise of Lorraine on a visit to the château. See Jean-Pierre Babelon and Christian Rémy, "Les châteaux de Bourdeilles," *Congrès archéologique de France, Périgord, 1999,* pp. 119-142. The mid-sixteenth-century château of Angerville-Bailleul has a central gallery leading to a straight staircase.

[23] J. Guillaume, 1969.

[24] The plan of the wooden model, reproduced by André Félibien, where the staircase is housed in one of the arms of the cross.

splendid scenery at every turning. An additional advantage of this disposition is that it allows for a passage between the two ground-floor chambers, along the bottom of that well of light twinned with a balcony overlooking the river.[21]

These unusual features of Chenonceau's plan, too unique to be imitated,[22] were analyzed seriously for the first time when Jean Guillaume examined its sources of inspiration.[23] After comparing it to a rare example of a raised plan with a central gallery, Martainville in Normandy (1485), and after considering the thinking surrounding the first designs for Chambord,[24] the author concluded that Chenonceau's plan has no equivalent in France. But, he acknowledges, if one

∧ The ceiling of the ground-floor vestibule-gallery.

∧ A medallion in the stairway vault.

accepts the notion that the choice of the castle's situation and interior design was guided first and foremost by the owner's desire to have it command views of the Cher throughout, one has to look at other possible sources of inspiration for this mansion on a river: the aquatic palaces of Venice. Thomas Bohier is known to have been in regular touch with the future doge Andrea Gritti, first when Gritti was a prisoner of the French at Milan in 1512 and later when he helped to negotiate the Franco-Venetian treaty of alliance at Blois on March 15, 1513. Two months later,

> The ground-floor
vestibule-gallery
with its zigzagging
vault crowns.
Before the
construction of
the bridge and
its galleries by
Diane de Poitiers
and Catherine
de' Medici the end
wall was a wide bay
provided with a
balcony overlooking
the Cher.

∧ The cloister of Saint-Martin de Tours by Bastien
François (Archives photographiques des Monuments historiques).

Gritti and Bohier traveled to Italy, and, in June of the same year, both were present at the defeat of Novara. Bohier may well have gleaned information about the architecture of Venetian palaces from his traveling companion; when he returned to the Touraine in 1514, he may even have brought back descriptions or plans of buildings along the Grand Canal, which feature a vast *salone* laid out to take full advantage of the view over the water.[25]

52

[25] J. Guillaume, 1969,
p. 39.
[26] This was the theory
of the abbé Chevalier
followed by R. Ranjard.
[27] First suggested by
C. Chevalier (notably
in his *Histoire de
Chenonceau*, p. 107),
this theory was again
put forward by
L. Palustre. F. Gebelin
refers to it in passing as
a "hazardous hypothesis"
(1927, p. 81).

Helped by his wife, Catherine, Thomas Bohier seems to have played a crucial part in Chenonceau's design, but we do not know who the master-builder was. Historians have naturally put forward the names of the contractors who worked at Amboise, Bury, Blois, Gaillon, Bonnivet, and Chambord, men like Colin Biart, Guillaume Senault, Pierre Nepveau or Trinqueau as he was called[26]—all three of whom appear to have been from Amboise. The vaulting of the vestibule at Chenonceau, with its amusing zigzag of intersecting ogee arches, and that of the stairway, a flattened barrel-vault reinforced with two sets of parallel ribs ornamented with medallions where they meet at right angles, recalls the vaulting in the Tour des Minimes at Amboise, the Louis XII stairs at Blois, and the cloister of Saint-Martin at Tours.

In view of all this one may advance the name of a family of architects and ornamental sculptors from Tours, the François brothers, Martin, Bastien, and Gatien, all nephews and pupils of Michel Colombe.[27] The elder was employed as early as 1491 on the construction of the Château of Amboise; later he worked at Gaillon

> The château chapel.
The entrance is
via the Salle des
gardes. The tall
windows with their
elegant moldings
were fitted with
stained-glass
by Max Ingrand
in 1954.

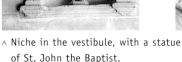
∧ Niche in the vestibule, with a statue of St. John the Baptist.

∧ ∧ Nero and Germanicus, two of the medallions adorning the walls of the second-floor vestibule-gallery.

[28] J. M. Pérouse de Montclos (ed.), *Le Guide du Patrimoine. Architectures en Region Centre,* Paris, 1987, with biographical notes on the artists by Bertrand Lemoine). For Bastien François, see Dr. Lesueur, "Saint-Martin de Tours," *Congrès archéologique de la France, Tours, 1948,* p. 25.

and, still later, at Tours on the cathedral, the Beaune-Semblançay fountain, and the Hôtel de la Bourdaisière. Bastien, the son-in-law of the great sculptor Guillaume Regnault and, in 1515, the king's master-mason in Touraine, was active at Amboise and the cathedral of Tours. The staircase at the cloister of La Psalette is attributed to him, and the handsome vaults of the Cloître Saint-Martin (1508-1519) are definitely his work. One of the brothers' fellow artisans, Pierre de Valence (who died in 1518), had worked at Gaillon as well before completing the left tower of Tours cathedral and, in 1507, contriving the hydraulic system of that city's fountains.[28] As mayor of Tours Thomas Bohier was certainly acquainted with all these skilled craftsmen and it would have been only natural for him to use their talents.

The quality of Chenonceau's sculpted decorations testifies to the gifts of the artisans who worked on the site. Initially closer to the Gothic sensibility, they appear, in a second phase of work, to have been inspired by the new language of the Italian models. The large dormers crowning the central bays, the bases

29 J. Guillaume, 2001,
p. 38. Guillaume directs
our attention particularly,
like L. Palustre earlier,
to the not very visible
frieze above the big
south dormer, with its
gesticulating band
of reveling fauns.

30 If it comes on time,
I'll remember it (trans.).

31 "Je ne doibs ma
grandeur qu'à ma fidélité"
(I owe my greatness to
my loyalty alone), in the
lofty translation in Guy
Bretonneau's *Histoire
généalogique de la maison
des Briçonnets,* 1620.

32 Speak well or be silent
(trans.).

of the vault and the stonework framing the doors in the vestibule, the carving
in the chapel and around the Marques' Tower door:[29] all show the hand
of supremely skilled craftsmen. The same standard of work is displayed in the
château's rooms, especially the library with its superb ceiling of geometrical
caissons in the Italian manner. Here again one encounters the initials TBK,
as well as the owner's strange motto, repeated several times elsewhere in the
castle, *S'il vient a point il me souviendra*,[30] which appears first on a Bohier coin
from 1503 and should presumably be read as a tax collector's pressing summons
to his taxpayers. These words recall another of the lord of Chenonceau's
apothegms, *Ditat servata fides*,[31] and the device of his in-laws the Briçonnets,
*Taire ou bien dire*,[32] all of them useful guidelines in an era of insecurity.

Bohier, who spent his last years in Italy, as we have said, had little leisure
to enjoy Chenonceau upon its completion. He died in 1524 and his body

∧ The ceiling of Thomas Bohier's
library, *ca.* 1525.

∧ ∧ Antique ceramic tiles grouped in the pavement
of the Salles des gardes, 1525.

33 The tomb was destroyed
in 1793 and we only
know of it through Guy
Bretonneau's description,
*op. cit.*

was brought back to Tours and buried in the church of Saint-Saturnin.
Two years later he was followed by his wife and a splendid tomb was erected
for them, a black marble slab supporting white marble effigies of the couple
kneeling in prayer carved by the illustrious brothers Juste.[33]

∧ The approach to the forecourt
and château.

> The Marques' Tower and west side
of the terrace moat.

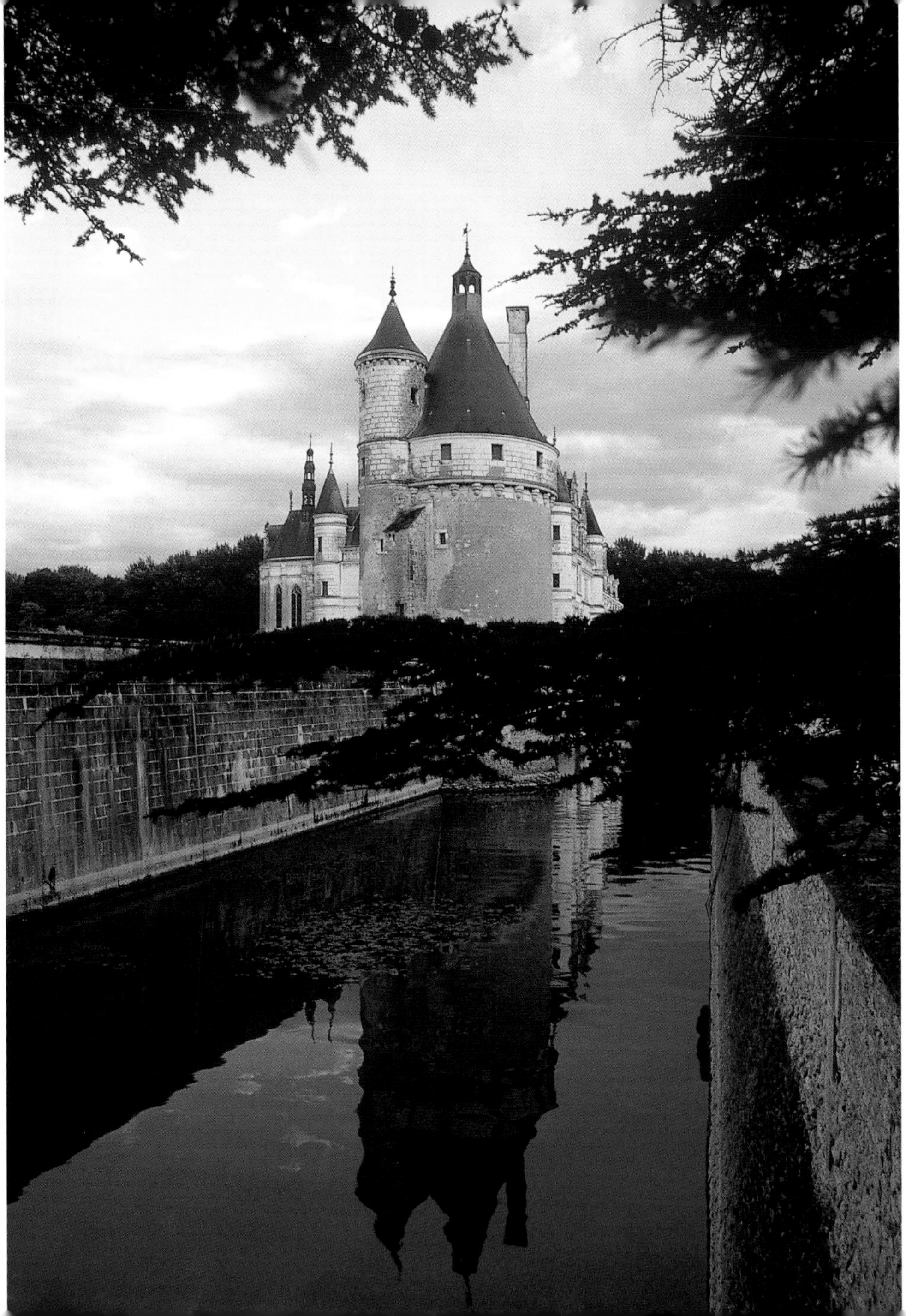

# 3

## DIANE DE POITIERS, THE KING'S FAVORITE, AT CHENONCEAU

| | |
|---|---|
| *Que voulez-vous, Diane bonne,* | *What cravest thou from me,* |
| *Que je vous donne?* | *Good Diane?* |
| *Vous n'eustes, comme j'entends,* | *They say thou never hadst such luck* |
| *Jamais tant d'heur au printemps* | *In springtime as thou hast now* |
| *Qu'en automne.* | *In Autumn.* |

Clément Marot, *Étrennes*, 1538

### A Hunting Rendezvous for Francis I

The Bohiers were survived by nine children. The eldest, Antoine, Baron of Saint-Ciergue and Governor of Touraine, and his wife Anne Poncher inherited Chenonceau. It was not a good time to come into that kind of property. Antoine had barely taken possession of the estate when, in 1527, Francis I set up his committee to root out embezzlers of public funds. In addition to Semblançay and Louis Poncher, Antoine's uncle and father-in-law, both of them hanged from the gibbet at Montfaucon, other persons close to Chenonceau's new master were investigated: his uncle Jean, his brother-in-law François, Bishop of Paris, who was to die in prison, and Gilles Berthelot, who would be sentenced to banishment. What is more, Antoine was ordered to make good the debts his father had incurred raising a new army at the time of the French debacle in the Duchy of Milan.

∧ *Francis I* by Jean and François Clouet (PARIS, MUSÉE DU LOUVRE).

The matter was argued back and forth for seven years, no less. Finally, in 1531, on the death of the formidable Louise of Savoy, Antoine was ordered to pay 190,000 *livres tournois*—a huge sum of money—to the royal treasury. Short of seeing the family ruined, the only option was to donate Chenonceau to the king. Francis I had had occasion to enjoy the château's charm—Chenonceau was the kind of hunting lodge he was particularly fond of— and, through the intervention of Anne de Montmorency, a deal was struck in 1535. The gift of the estate took care of 90,000 *livres* of the debt. To this Antoine Bohier had to add an extra 60,000 *livres* in cash. Once this was paid, the family was discharged from paying the remainder on the "king's word and good faith."

On coming into possession of the castellany, Francis I appointed the royal treasurer at Tours, Philibert Babou de La Bourdaisière, to oversee it. However he did not bother to have the castle furnished. Thus Chenonceau became merely another of the royal court's temporary haunts. We know of two regal visits in particular: one in August 1538, when the king came with his wife Eleanor of Austria and his mistress, the Duchess of Étampes; and another in the spring of 1545, around the time when Francis I was nursing his ailments and sorrows at Plessis-lès-Tours and his retinue was trying to keep him entertained. A hunting party was organized on the banks of the Cher. The Dauphin Henri was there, almost certainly accompanied by Diane de Poitiers.

63

*Diane de Poitiers*, 2<sup>e</sup> femme de Louis de Brézé Grand Senechal de Normandie, créée Duchesse de Valentinois par Henri II en 1548.

LA·GRANT·SENECHALLE

∧ *Diane de Poitiers*. Three-pencil portrait (BIBLIOTHÈQUE NATIONALE DE FRANCE, CABINET DES ESTAMPES).

Diane was thus well acquainted with Chenonceau by the time Francis I's death at Rambouillet, on March 31, 1547, made her France's *grande favorite*, the supreme mistress of the new monarch's power, favor, and pleasures. Her éclat all but overshadowed Queen Catherine de' Medici. Such was her beauty, said poets, that it defied the passing years—she was forty-eight then—and her wit, forceful personality, not to say her rapacity, had long held the prince, now King Henry II, in thrall. Ostentatiously dressed in mourning for her late husband, Louis de Brézé, grand seneschal of Normandy, "la Grande Sénéchale," as she was universally called, was given the Duchy of Valentinois by the king. In addition, her domain at Anet, which had been placed under sequestration, was returned to her and, in a letter patent of June 1547, she was deeded the château of Limours, confiscated from the Duchess of Etampes, and the château of Chenonceau.

Diane, who was shrewd in legal matters, wanted to make certain that she would never be dispossessed of Chenonceau as Francis I's favorite had been dispossessed of Limours. This meant establishing that Chenonceau was her personal property, not simply a royal domain placed at her disposal, and this in turn involved having the transaction of 1535 nullified and proven fraudulent. Notwithstanding the former king's pledge, a writ was served on the unfortunate Antoine Bohier in 1550 on the grounds that he had overvalued the estate. His defense arguments went unheeded and he had to flee to Venice, perhaps to the hospitality of his father's friends, even before the case went before the Grand Council presided by Henry II. The king, who was simultaneously judge and plaintiff, was bent on pleasing his mistress. And so the case was tried *in absentia*, leaving the voluntary exile no choice but to consent in writing, on December 21, 1553, to the annulment of the sale of 1535 and hence to his reinstatement as owner. As a result all his property was auctioned off to repay his "debt" to the royal treasury. Chenonceau was sequestered, put up for sale—and sold to Diane de Poitiers on June 8, 1555, for the sum of 50,000 *livres*, which sum she of course never paid.[34] Even before the sale was finalized, la Grande Sénéchale took possession of Chenonceau and started collecting revenues from the estate to pay for remodeling the château.

### Diane's Parterre

Diane first turned her attention to the castle grounds. By the 1550s the art of laying out gardens had come to claim as great a place in the hearts of Renaissance lords as architecture, painting, and sculpture. King René of Anjou had set the trend in the previous century, and with Charles VIII's Italian incursion

[34] C. Chevalier, *Archives royales de Chenonceau,* vol. V.

64

>
One of the buildings of the La Grange tenant farm.

and the revelation of Italy's fountains, pruned trees, shady bowers, and flower beds rich as embroidery—and chiefly, perhaps, her fragrances and blue skies—the vogue for gardens had become something of a craze. From Naples King Charles brought back the illustrious horticulturist Pacella da Mercogliano and immediately put him to work at Amboise. Later, Louis XII had da Mercogliano design the gardens at Blois on the hill across from the royal château.

The Bohiers too followed the fashion. After all, horticulture provided a way of upgrading the estate's farmland. Chenonceau included a great variety of terrains, pastures, fields, hemp plantations, abundant vineyards, woodland, tracts of heather, and warrens. Close to the castle were three parks totaling some 90 hectares (220 acres), named after the parishes they bordered: Francueil on the left bank of the river and on the right bank, to either side of the avenue leading to the château, Civray and Chisseau,

South of the tenant farm of La Grange, several interesting buildings of which survive, the Parc de Civray encompassed a number of other service structures connected to the Pavillon des Marques. There Bohier had erected a chapel to his patron saint, St Thomas, which was later renamed the Chapelle Saint-Hubert or Chapelle du Pavillon. To this string of "small houses," Diane in 1551 had her mason Pierre Hurlu add quarters for her officers. Behind them there was a garden known as the Jardin du Pavillon. Here Diana commissioned a carpenter from Amboise named Jean Rasteau to construct a quadrangle of latticed grape arbors around a basin. Vineyards were already the pride of the estate and have remained so ever since. The park was adorned and illuminated for Henri II's visits in 1549 and 1552. A fifteen-acre tree nursery and a one-acre kitchen garden adjoined it then.

These early gardens, like those of Blois and Gaillon, were laid out a good way off from the castle though directly in view of it, and one had to walk a certain distance to reach them. Exiting from the château onto the Marques' terrace, one turned left and crossed the moat on a steep wooden ramp on piles. This passageway is perfectly visible on two of Du Cerceau's drawings (reproduced on p. 80), as is an elaborately architectural gate leading to it on the flank of the great tower.[35]

But such a modest garden could not long satisfy the Duchess of Valentinois. She soon set her sights on a two-and-a-half acre barley field on the bank of the Cher to the left of the terrace. It seemed an ideal site for a parterre large enough to give her scope to show off her superior taste. However, it was exposed to the Cher's sometimes violent floods[36] and had to be protected by a massive earth embankment with steeply-angled sides reinforced with masonry. A moat fed by the river was dug around three sides of the embankment, while the Cher washed the fourth side. On the south-east corner a floodgate was built and a catwalk was later erected above it, making it possible to control flooding. At the corner closest to the castle's forecourt a wooden bridge provided the only access to the parterre. Earlier, at Azay-le-Rideau,[37] Gilles Berthelot and his wife had laid out a garden on an artificial island in the Indre, reached from the Château by a bridge spanning a moat teeming with fish. Diane's parterre was a veritable bastion encircled with water, and it suited the Marques' feudal platform.

An unbroken succession of terraces flanked by parapets looked over the parterre, which was fully visible as well from the apartments and the small terrace on the east side of the château. This wholly-enclosed corner of paradise contained flower beds, an orchard, and a kitchen garden—for the useful and the delightful had not

[35] The estate's accounts for 1554-1555 mention making a key for "the door to the tower ramp." C. Chevalier, *Archives royales,* vol. II, p. 183. In the seventeenth century the wooden bridge was replaced by a stone bridge which was torn down in 1870 on Madame Pelouze's orders, for she thought it spoiled "the *donjon*'s imposing isolation."

[36] In April 1555, an unusually severe flood damaged the parterre's plantations and masonry.

[37] Jean-Claude Le Guillou, *Azay-le-Rideau. Entre Renaissance et Romantisme,* Paris: CNMHS, 1995.

69

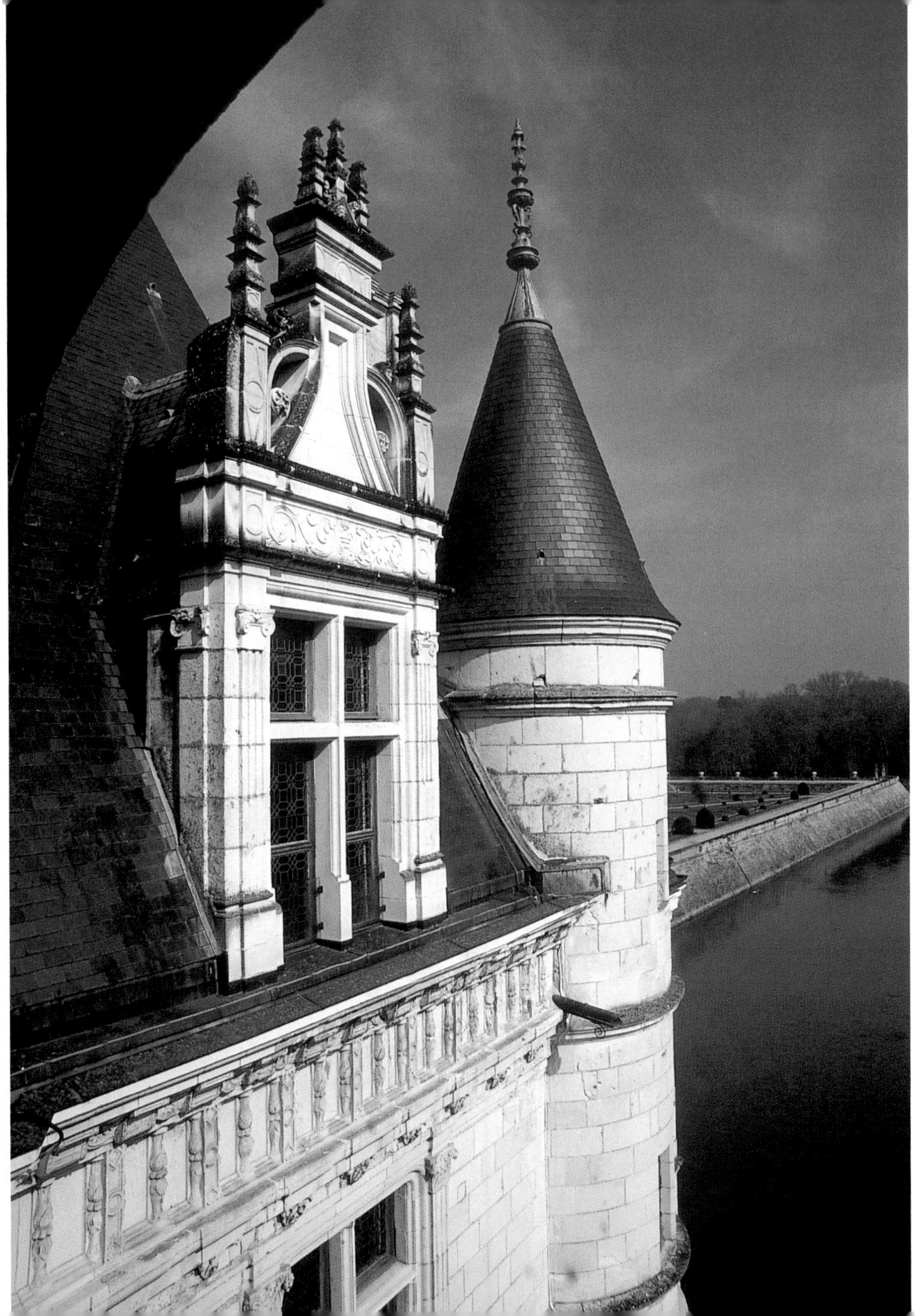

< A dormer on the south façade.

∧ Diane's parterre resembling a fortified bastion
opposite the Marques' terrace. The Pavillon
de la Chancellerie is on the left.

yet become separate realms: witness the gardens at Villandry. Contracted in April 1551, the terracing and masonry work on the parterre platform continued into the winter of 1554. The moats were dug and edged with masonry in 1556-1557.[38]

The parterre was planted as the work on the embankment was still underway. Diane consulted the finest garden connoisseurs in the area: the archbishop of Tours, who had a wonderful garden at Vernou, and, chiefly, the abbé de Pontlevoy, Bernard de Ruthie, *grand aumonier* of the kingdom whom Diane appointed her *procureur général,* or superintendent. The abbé sent her his steward, Benoît Guy, *sieur* des Carroys; Archbishop Simon de Maillé sent her his vicar general, Jean de Selve, the abbot of Turpenay, as well has the latter's gardener; and many other personages made gifts to la Grande Sénéchale. Willow trees were planted on the terrace and along the paths, and white mulberries, for Diane was eager to breed silk worms and thereby encourage the development of sericulture in Tours. Every variety of fruit tree was brought in as well: apple trees, pear trees, plum trees, cherry trees, peach trees, and shrubs to make hedge borders, hawthorns and hazelnut trees, all under the watchful eye of an orchard specialist from Tours named Nicquet. The kitchen garden had redcurrants and strawberry beds, artichokes, onions, cabbages, leeks, vegetables of every sort, and the flower beds brimmed with lovely blossoms like the ones Clément Marot sang in 1515 in his poem *Cupido*:

> *Marguerites, lys et oeillets,*
> *Passevelouz, roses flairantes;*
> *Romarins, boutons vermeilletz,*
> *Lavandes odoriférantes.*[39]

Judging from the drawings Du Cerceau executed not long after, between 1559 and 1565, the paths laid out in 1552 crossed each other at right angles,

[38] C. Chevalier, *Archives royales,* vol. III, no. XXIII.

[39] Daisies, lilies, and sweet william/Amaranths, fragrant roses/Rosemary, crimson buds,/Odorous lavender (trans.).

[40] The original arrangement can be seen on an engraving by Dupin de Franceuil and on a plan touched up with watercolors by Dupas de la Chauvinière, dated 1735, reproduced on pp. 128 and 175. The Muller lithograph after Roguet that illustrates C. Chevalier's brief 1869 article shows a crosslike plan with regular triangular divisions in each of the four compartments divided by paths intersecting to form an X.

[41] Cardin de Valence's fountain has inspired Arnaud de Saint-Jouan's fountain recently built on the same spot (2002).

[42] C. Chevalier, *Archives royales de Chenonceau*, vol. II, pp. 136 and 291, which mentions two visits by "Monsieur de Saint-Germain," whom the Abbé Chevalier identifies as a *gentilhomme* named Julien de Saint-Germain. We know that Philibert de l'Orme was the curé and temporal lord of Saint-Germain at Châtres sous Montlhéry, a title later transferred to his brother and collaborator, Jean de l'Orme. See J. M. Pérouse de Montclos, pp. 64-65.

creating four rectangular partitions divided by narrower paths into quadrangles of lawn. Today's X-shaped plan was laid out in the late nineteenth century.[40] The parterre required a large hydraulic system. Cardin de Valence, a fountain master from Tours and the grandson of Pierre de Valence we mentioned earlier, was commissioned to build it. To feed the basins and the fountain at the intersection of the parterre's paths, water was piped in from the fountainhead of La Roche and the spring of La Dagrenière. The fountain itself was a six-inch "rock" with a hole plugged by a wooden stopper. When the stopper is removed, Du Cerceau writes, "there gushes forth a jet of water three *toises* [18 feet] high, which is a pretty and pleasing device."[41]

So original is Diane de Poitiers' parterre and so skillfully blended with the château and the river that it can only have been designed by a supreme landscape artist. And indeed Diane had at hand the best designer in France, Philibert de l'Orme. De l'Orme had been the Dauphin's and, after 1547, King Henry's architect and had already worked for the Grande Sénéchale. A few years earlier (1548-1553), he had built her château at Anet, the gem of the new French architecture. Moreover, since 1548 he had been sharing with her the revenues from the Abbey of Ivry, which she had obtained for him. He may have visited Chenonceau as early as December 1551 and January 1552,[42] on the latter occasion to request advance payment from Diane de Poitiers "for making the gallery from the castle to the aforesaid garden," a project that came to nothing. On the other hand, we are certain of his presence at the castle under the name "Monsieur d'Ivry," from 1556 on, at which time he paid the fountain builder for his work. The bastion-like design of Diane's parterre is unquestionably in the architect's style, for Philibert de l'Orme was an acknowledged master at building defense works.

73

∧ The entrance avenue presently flanked by plane trees.

∧ The canal bordering the avenue.

[43] Le Plessis, *Les Triomphes faictz à l'entrée du roy à Chenonceau le dymanche dernier jour de mars*, Tours: Guillaume Bourgeat, 1560 (new style), reprinted by A. Galitzin, Paris, 1857.

But having this splendid carpet of flowers and shrubs beneath the windows of her bed-chamber was still not enough for Diane. She also wanted to embellish the approach to the château. In early 1557, it seems, she had an elm-lined avenue laid out in the axis of the castle entrance: "The main avenue to this castle is a broad sandy road laid out as a graceful garden *allée*, about thirty paces wide and two miles long, the sides of which are enclosed by tall elms, evergreen oaks, and other fine trees."[43] The ground immediately around the castle was cleared and a spacious esplanade of elms was planted, with a wide path leading to the parterre bridge. Diane ordered the uncultivated tract adjoining the parterre to the north to be landscaped as well: sandy walks were traced, bowers were built, a *dedalus*—or maze—was designed, and a pall-mall alley and other outdoor games areas were laid out. In short, the new gardens offered all the fashionable amusements and amenities of the age. This landscaping did not cost Diane very much, for in a letter patent dated January 17, 1552, Henry II granted her 5,500 *livres* from the revenues of the *sénéchausée* of Les Landes in gratitude for the "agreeable and commendable" services she was rendering "to our most dear and beloved companion the Queen." As the shrewd proprietor of a rich estate, Diane, eager to increase its territory, acquired the seigniory of Chisseau and its four fiefs bordering Chenonceau.

## Diane's Bridge

The country on the south bank of the Cher, toward Franceuil, was hillier and prettier. At the foot of the hills there were meadows washed by the Vestin, which fed a couple of fountains and drove several mill wheels. It looked ideal for planting more gardens, but the only way to get there was by boat.

Philibert de l'Orme, from whom the Grande Sénéchale got her ideas, drew a vertical line from north to south in the axis of the new avenue. Running down the length of Thomas Bohier's vestibule-gallery, it extended through the bay opposite the entrance and across the river. The solution, then, was nothing less than a bridge, an audacious plan that could not fail to appeal to Diane. The architect was present at Chenonceau in the beginning of 1556; with him was a master-mason from Montrichard named Pierre Hurlu, who was already at work on the site. De l'Orme had him probe the bed of the Cher, which turned out to be rocky enough to support a row of piers, between which the boats that plied the river would have to navigate. An island formed by the head of a stone dam, which had been built earlier to channel the water toward the former mill, was removed in January 1558 to free the current.

∧ The château and the bridge-gallery
from the east.

> South view of the alignment of semi-circular
turrets built for Catherine de' Medici above
the tips of the piers of Diane's bridge.

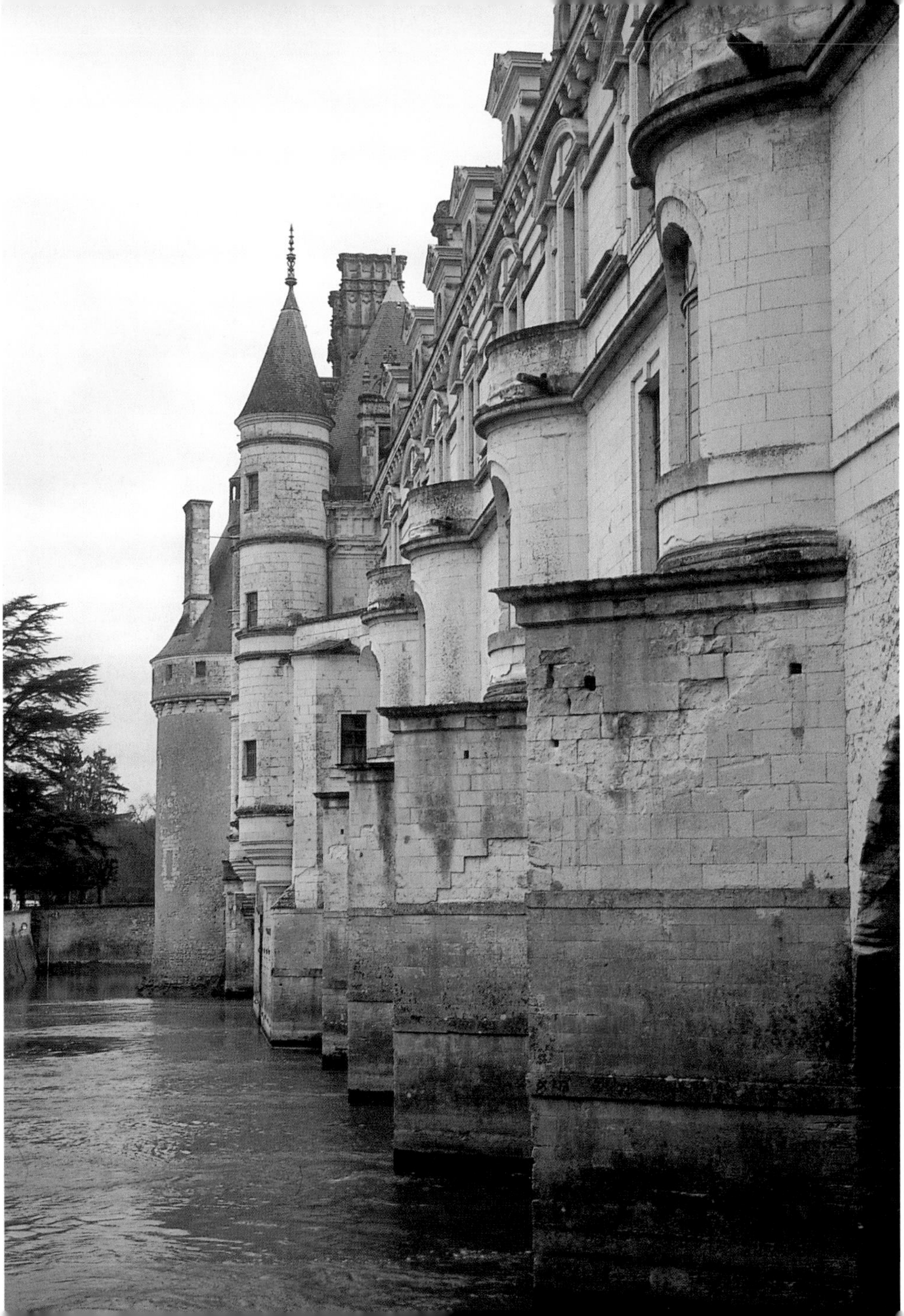

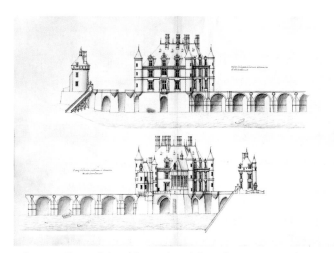

∧ Cross-sections of the château viewed from downstream and
upstream. Drawing by Du Cerceau, *ca.* 1560 (LONDON, BRITISH MUSEUM).
Diane's bridge is shown as yet without a parapet.

44 Thanks to the surviving
estimates and accounting
records, it is possible to
reconstruct in detail the
progress of the work.
C. Chevalier, *Archives
royales,* vol. III and
certain records in vol. II.
45 C. Chevalier, *Archives
royales,* vol. III,
document III, which
I have collated with
the original.

An initial contract for the work
was drawn up and signed
on April 2, 1556, followed
eight days later by a second
agreement for construction
of the caissons for laying
the foundations of the piers.[44]
This provided yet another
opportunity for Henry II to
oblige his mistress by donating
about fifty oak trees from
the forest of Montrichard
for building the caissons
and the frames for erecting the arches. The original plan called for seven piers
to be constructed. Directed by Philibert's brother, Jean de l'Orme, the work
began immediately under the authority of the overseer of Diane's household.
Judging from an anxious letter of Philibert's, dated July 18, 1556, there
were difficulties almost from the first. It became apparent that Hurlu,
who was probably in poor health, was not cut out for the job. A stone dresser
named Jean Philippon, or Jean de Vienne, was hired to assist him. Hurlu died
shortly after December 5. Philippon was paid for his work and on July 27,
1557, a survey was made to determine what had been accomplished so far.
Jacques Coqueau of Amboise, the controller of the royal buildings at Blois
and Pierre Trinqueau's successor at Chambord, wrote an assessment
of the work completed, listed what remained to be done, and engaged
the services of two new masons, one from Paris, the other from Blois:
Jacques Le Blanc and Claude Lenfant.

This document of July 1557[45] is of crucial importance, for it describes
Philibert's project in detail. An extra pier was added to the south of the four
that had already been built by this date, almost 16 feet (4.85 m.) long
and constructed of hard stone from Chisseau and Les Houdes, whereupon work
commenced on building five arches of tender Bourré, Saint-Aignan, and Lie
dressed stone. In spite of the different widths of the arches, resulting from
Hurlu's miscalculations, the keystones were all to be aligned at the same height.
The tips of the piers facing upstream were tapered "to give strength to the said
bridge," except for that of the central pier, which was to have "two concave
overhangs on the round tower in order to gain between nine and twelve feet
on each side"—in other words it was to have a half-turret on each of its two
sides. The structure's form was to harmonize with the semicircular balconies
of Bohier's castle. Eight iron rings were affixed to the piers, for mooring boats.

The bridge, however, was not just a means for crossing the Cher, it was part of the
castle and was designed to extend its capacity by providing an element lacking
in the modest manor-houses of the early sixteenth century: a gallery. Combining
the functions of a passageway, a banquet hall, and a ballroom, galleries had begun
to appear in every sizable château in France. Francis I's castle at Fontainebleau
already boasted a gallery that was a masterpiece of Renaissance architecture.
Obviously Henry II's favorite mistress could not receive the royal court without
having her own gallery. Philibert de l'Orme designed a system for her like that
which his colleague Jean Bullant was then building to expand and modernize the
Château de Fère-en-Tardenois by spanning the ravine encircling the old stronghold
belonging to the king's favorite, Anne de Montmorency, with a gallery-bridge.
Actually, an older and closer precedent existed, the Galerie des Cerfs at Blois,
begun under Louis XII, to provide a passage between the château and the gardens.

46 In an article written in 1993, Jean Guillaume showed that Du Cerceau's engraved plan (reproduced p. 48) erroneously blocked off the vestibule's visual axis. I have also concluded that it is mistaken about the width of the bridge (which it gives as 25 feet). I will thus not repeat Guillaume's theory concerning a plan to have two outside terraces running on either side of a gallery narrower than the bridge.

47 This drawing was acquired on the art market by the château's curator some twenty years ago. A similar drawing, having a broader field of vision, exists at the Bibliothèque Nationale de France, cabinet des Estampes, Ve 26 k (coll. Destailleur). It is reproduced by R. A. Weigert. The fortified gate is also clearly visible on one of Dupin de Francueil's engravings, dated 1739, reproduced on p. 175.

The gallery at Chenonceau was designed to be as wide (18 feet, or 5.85 m.) as the 197-foot (60-m.) bridge. It abuts the castle's rear façade, slightly downstream from the center so as not to block the view from the vestibule which ends, as we have said, in front of a balcony. The balcony itself was extended laterally to give access to the bridge.[46] A room designed to serve as a pantry was fitted out on this side and connected with the castle's basement kitchen; it is now used as a butcher's room.

A simple one-story structure between walls eight feet high (2.60 m.) aligned with the arches, the gallery was conceived to be lit on both sides by windows 12 feet (1.45 m.) wide and almost 10 feet (3 m.) high jutting out above the tapered ends of the piers. These tall casements were to project over the cornice and the roof, after the new manner de l'Orme had already experimented with at Anet and that Bullant would use at Chantilly. Not being intended to provide a passage to the south bank, the gallery led to a French window slightly over 5 feet wide (1.60 m.), opening onto a balcony overhanging the last pier, which was to serve as "a terrace to go out on and breathe fresh air." A plan for an extra, optional pier on which a drawbridge could be erected was considered. The pier below the balcony was to support a couple of small lateral projecting pavilions for housing privies, a wardrobe, and a spiral staircase leading down to the river. Finally, the gallery was to be heated by two small chimneys.

Lenfant and Le Blanc continued the work on the bridge, but by the end of the summer Le Blanc no longer gave satisfaction and Philibert de l'Orme replaced him with one of his customary collaborators, Jacques Chanterel. A contract was drawn up with the latter on September 5. On September 23, de l'Orme gave instructions in writing for Chanterel to be paid 500 *livres* as an advance on a 6000-*livre* budget.

By then there was no longer any question of building anything more elaborate than a bridge. The notations on Chanterel and Lenfant's successive receipts contain no mention of a gallery. Chanterel died toward the end of the summer of 1558 and a new mason, Jean Norays of Loches, is mentioned by name on a document dated January 27 of the following year. Much remained to be done—even the arches were unfinished—and the fateful year when the ownership of Chenonceau passed from Diane to Queen Catherine de' Medici had commenced. Then yet another setback: a wooden frame for building an arch collapsed into the river, and put a sudden stop to the work. This is the state of affairs—a bridge with no gallery ending with a turreted gate and drawbridge—depicted in an ink-and-wash drawing entitled

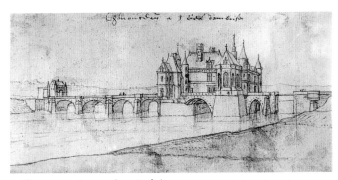

∧ *Chenonceau 3 Leagues from Amboise.* Anonymous ink-and-wash, *ca.* 1560 (Château de Chenonceau). The gate tower defending the bridge to the left bank is visible on the left.

*Chenonceau a 3 lieus damboise* in the Château archives.[47] The small balconies overlooking the pier buttresses are not semicircular but uniformly rectangular, a design apparent on Du Cerceau's drawings and engravings as well.[48]

Despite the importance of the work being undertaken at Chenonceau, Diane de Poitiers spent little time there. It lay too far from the castles where Henry II was now sojourning further north. However she did receive the king, the queen, and the court at the château on several occasions, notably for a lavish celebration in the spring of 1552. Diane preferred the castle Philibert de l'Orme had designed

[48] The bridge does not even have a parapet on Du Cerceau's drawn cross-sections. However, the parapet and rectangular balconies appear on the later engravings.

85

>

The château's west façade. The windows of the central bay supply light to the main staircase.

for her at Anet and kept a more watchful eye on the work in progress there. Yet her ties with the Touraine were still strong: keenly interested in wine-growing, she purchased good land for vineyards on the heights of Amboise and even contemplated having a small residence built there with a direct passage to the royal castle allowing her to visit Henry II when he was present.

The dramatic tournament of the rue Saint-Antoine in Paris[49] shattered the prospects of the young king's mistress and she now found herself in the same position as the Duchess of Étampes upon Francis I's death. On July 10, 1559, she was barred from entering the room where the king lay dying. She was nothing now. Her loyal ally Montmorency was banished from the Court. Fearing confiscation, Diane hastily returned the jewels the king had given her. Now Catherine de' Medici had always loved Chenonceau, which she had visited several times, and was determined to uphold the royal prerogative over the castellany. Diane, who had sought from the very first to have it registered as her personal property, countered that, as it did not belong to the Crown, it could not be taken back.

Queen Catherine soon changed tack and proposed a trade to Diane. For Chenonceau, she announced, she was willing to give up Chaumont, a château originally belonging to the d'Amboise family, which she had acquired in 1550. Diane held out briefly and then reluctantly agreed: she had no option and from a financial standpoint it was not a bad arrangement. The estate of Chaumont was worth a third more than the land at Chenonceau. The act was signed toward the end of the year at the château de Blois in the presence of the adolescent King Francis II.[50] Thereupon the former royal mistress retired from Court and divided the remaining six years of her life between her castles at Limours[51] and Anet. She died at Anet at the age of 66 on April 25, 1566, and was buried there.

# 4

| | |
|---|---|
| *Qui vous tient doncq si loin de nous, Madame?* | *What keeps you so far from us, Madam?* |
| *C'est le désir de consumer la flame* | *It is the desire to put out the flame* |
| *Qui peut rester des civiles fureurs,* | *Of civil fury perhaps still raging* |
| *Et nettoyer nos provinces d'erreurs.* | *And to cleanse our provinces of error.* |
| *Vostre vouloir soit fait à la bonne heure;* | *May your will be carried early,* |
| *Mais retournez en la saison meilleure,* | *But come back to us in a milder season,* |
| *Et faites voir au retour du printemps* | *And with spring's return show us* |
| *De vostre front tous vos peuples contents.* | *A face that contents all your people.* |
| *Vostre Monceaux tout gaillard vous appelle,* | *Your gallant Monceau calls you,* |
| *Sainct-Maur pour vous fait sa rive plus belle,* | *Saint Maur makes its banks lovelier,* |
| *Et Chenonceau rend pour vous diaprez* | *For you Chenonceau scatters* |
| *De mille fleurs son rivage et ses prez;* | *A thousand blossoms over its meadows and banks.* |
| *La Tuillerie au bastiment superbe* | *And La Tuilerie's splendid edifice* |
| *Pour vous fait croistre et son bois et son herbe,* | *Makes its woods and lawns increase* |
| *Et désormais ne désire sinon* | *And desires nothing more henceforth* |
| *Que d'enrichir son front de vostre nom.* | *Than to enrich its front with your name.* |

Pierre de Ronsard, *Le Bocage royal. À la reine Catherine*, 1563

## The Triumphs

When Henry II died Francis II was only fifteen-and-a-half-years old. Though he had attained the age at which the kings of France were legally entitled to reign and was already married to Mary Stuart, the beautiful Queen of Scotland, he was too young to govern and the power remained in the hands of his mother. As regent, Catherine de' Medici found herself confronted with the great problem of the age, religious strife. She tried at first to make peace between the opposing factions, but the princes of royal blood and the reformed nobility bore ill the intolerance of the Catholic faction led by the young queen's uncles, the Duke of Guise and the Cardinal of Lorraine, who controlled the royal council. Before long a plot was hatched to wrest the young king from their influence. It was quickly exposed and ruthlessly suppressed. The court retreated to the royal stronghold of Amboise, where it could be warned of approaching enemies. The conspirators were captured in small groups and hung from the town's gallows and even from the balcony of the royal apartments. Thus began, in March 1560, the hostilities that were to bloody France for more than three decades.

∧ *Queen Catherine de' Medici as a widow.*
Detail from a painting commissioned by Madame Pelouze for the fireplace of the main downstairs bed-chamber.

An old hand at organizing festivals to preserve the royal authority in times of crisis, Queen Catherine decided that her new castle, only a short ride from Amboise, was an ideal setting for lavish celebrations she hoped would appease inflamed passions. A first fête was given on Sunday, March 31, 1560, merely a few days after the plot was quelled. It provided the Queen Mother with an opportunity for organizing a pageant like the royal entrances of the French kings into Paris after their coronation at Rheims. We know every detail of the "triumphs" of Francis II and Mary Stuart.[52] Processing through the forest where the last of the conspirators were perhaps still being hunted down, the court *au grand complet* was led by the king and queen, the Guises, the Prince de Condé (who had masterminded the plot and was being held under close surveillance), the Colignys, Diane de Poitiers' son-in-law the Duke d'Aumale, and a huge retinue.

Organized jointly by the queen's steward and the château's captain, the festivities' real impresario, the man who made the statues and designed the costumes, was the illustrious Italian painter Francesco Primaticcio, recently promoted to the rank of Superintendent of Buildings at Chenonceau following the disgrace of Diane's architect, Philibert de l'Orme. The leading court poets Ronsard, Dorat, Baïf, and Jodelle were asked to contribute the inevitably rather sententious mottos and inscriptions without which no Renaissance fête was complete. Triumphal arches, columns, obelisks, gushing fountains, and neo-Classical altars were erected here and there on the château's grounds.

As the royal couple drew near, nine hundred costumed and flag-waving artisans and peasants from the estate went to meet them. The cortège then moved on down the main avenue decked with flowers, to the forecourt (where Catherine de' Medici

93

∧ *Execution of conspirators at the château of Amboise in March 1560.* I. Tortorel and J. Périssin, woodblock for *Les Histoires diverses... des guerres, massacres et troubles advenus en France.*

[52] Le Plessis, *Les Triomphes, op. cit.*(see note 43). The author notes that when the château doors stood open one had a view clear through the castle to a "second castle" across the river, *i.e.* the fortified gate at the south end of the bridge.

∧ The Salle des gardes.

∧ The main ground-floor bed-chamber, successively occupied by the Bohiers, Diane
de Poitiers, and Catherine de' Medici. The fireplace after the manner of Jean Goujon
was reconstructed under the Villeneuves and then modified for Madame Pelouze.

was later to have stone lions installed, later replaced by sphinxes). A triumphal arch with ivy twined round its columns greeted them with mottos praising the "divine Francis" and extolling his victory over the conspirators. Further on, two fountains topped by colossal busts on tapering pillars spouted water from golden gargoyles. "Do not muddy this water," ran the verses accompanying them, "O Passerby, for 'tis the water/ That is brought to Chenonceau/ For everyone to drink from." Last of all came two large oak trees decked with canisters of blazing oil, flanked by obelisks covered with Greek inscriptions.

∧ *A Royal Ball.* Anonymous painting, *ca.* 1580 (MUSÉE DE BLOIS).

The king walked over the bridge to the Terrace of the Marques and paused briefly to gaze at the fish glimmering in the moat under the glow of fireworks. From the terrace one could survey the whole site as if one were seated on a horse. In one corner a "lychnophore," a sort of lighthouse, lit up the château, the courtyards, and the gardens; in the other corner an antique altar celebrated the glory of the Queen Mother, and on the terrace's south side stood a Corinthian triumphal arch. Welcomed by salvos of artillery, Francis II approached the raised drawbridge, which was adorned with a personification of Fame. The bridge was lowered—"Bowing to Your Majesty's sole greatness"—and the king entered the château under a shower of bouquets and garlands scattered by a girl attired as the goddess Pallas: "King of the

French," went the verses commenting on this tableau, "from the skies where
thy father dwells,/ I, Pallas, have come to show thee/ This rural retreat
I am having redone/ To serve thee one day as a royal dwelling."

For Catherine de' Medici wanted Chenonceau to become a royal residence like
the palace of the Tuileries in Paris. Yet in the eyes of her contemporaries it was
only a "small house" at best suitable "for laying out gardens and other objects
of pleasure."[53] It was at all events a peaceful retreat, a place for Catherine
to rest in and reflect, in a tragic age. It was far from Paris, Saint-Germain,
and Fontainebleau where armed conflict was a daily reality. And it was a place
of pleasure, where she could receive the "Ladies' Court" established by Anne
de Bretagne, to which she herself, using the high-born women of her entourage
to advance her policies, added considerable brilliance. Three hundred maidens
and ladies surrounded her permanently and the King's quartermasters
complained that the Queen Mother's female retinue occupied half of the royal
household and attracted an equal number of gentlemen.

On Francis II's premature death in December 1560 the crown was again placed
on the head of a minor, Charles IX. Catherine was named regent, gaining an
even tighter grasp of the reins of power. When peace was made with the Prince
de Condé in March 1563, ending the first war of religion, Catherine returned
to Chenonceau with her three sons and her daughter Marguerite. She was eager
to see how the work on the gardens was progressing. Once again festivities
were organized: a ballet of nymphs and satyrs, a *pastorale,* boat outings on the
river, and, as always, hunting.[54] Two years later, in December 1565, as a special
event in the court's grand tour of France, Catherine organized a new triumph
for Charles IX at Chenonceau, which lasted four days.

[53] Letter from the Spanish
ambassador Chantonnay
to the Duchess of Parma,
March 23, 1560. See
Gebelin (1927), p. 83.

[54] See Comte Boulay
de la Meurthe,
"Entrée de Charles IX
à Chenonceau,"
*Mémoires de la Société
archéologique de
Touraine,* vol. 41, 1900,
pp. 151-190.

97

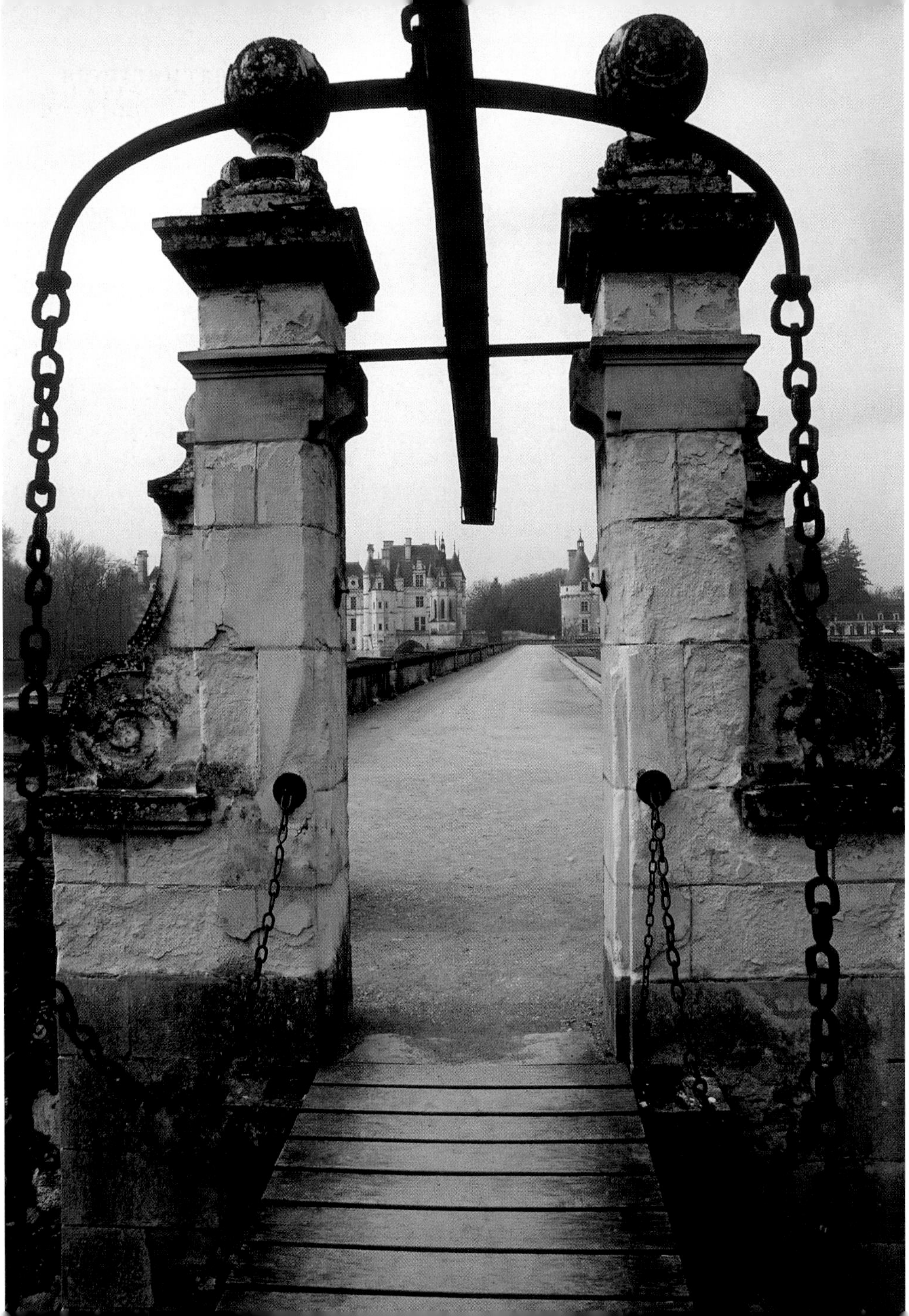

< The drawbridge to Diane's parterre from
the right bank of the Cher.

∧ The Pavillon de la Chancellerie and
a landing stage for boats.

Of Catherine de' Medici's numerous sojourns at Chenonceau, one in particular deserves notice, for it took place on the eve of the massacre of the Huguenots on Saint Bartholomew's Day, 1572. As the negotiations for the marriage of Marguerite de Valois to Henry of Navarre were proving delicate, Henry's mother, Jeanne d'Albret, set out in spite of her illness to join the royal court at Blois. Catherine asked her to come to Chenonceau on February 15, hoping to bring her around to her views. Marguerite de Valois was there, "beautiful and sensible and gracious," furthering her mother's arguments with her charm and wiles against which Jeanne d'Albret proved defenseless.

100

∧ *Welcoming the Polish Ambassadors at the Jardin des Tuileries, September 14, 1573*. Tapestry after a cartoon by Antoine Caron, 1582-1585 (FLORENCE, UFFIZI). Henry III stands on the left and Catherine de' Medici is seated in the background.

On May 30, 1574, only two years after the slaughter and wedding, Charles IX died and Henry III acceded to the throne. For her favorite son, the Queen Mother organized a third triumph at the château. The pretext this time was the victory of the king's last surviving brother, the Duke of Anjou, over the Huguenot stronghold of La Charité-sur-Loire, to the rejoicing of the Catholic party supported by the League. After a first feast at Plessis-lès-Tours, a banquet in honor of the two princes was held on May 15, 1577, in the new garden at Chenonceau near the Fontaine du Rocher. Catherine de' Medici was flanked by Marguerite de Valois and

Louise of Lorraine, the Queens of Navarre and France, accompanied by their maids of honor. The guests were served by ladies of the court naked from the waist up and wearing their hair loose. As for Henry III, this was the time when he generally appeared at court celebrations dressed in women's clothes, wearing a pearl necklace and triple linen collars over a doublet open at the neck, surrounded by a flock of pomaded boys in make-up and wearing their hair in curls.[55] The entertainments, which almost certainly included performances by *gelosi*, the fashionable actors the queen was fond of summoning from Venice, cost close to 100,000 *livres*, if we are to believe Pierre de L'Estoile. The day after the festival the Duke of Anjou left for the Auvergne where, on June 2, he captured the Huguenot town of Issoire. The report of this victory so delighted Henry III, who had stayed behind at Chenonceau, that he proposed renaming the château "Bonnes Nouvelles" (Good Tidings).

Catherine frequently returned to Chenonceau: it was her favorite residence. In 1578, she again received her daughter Marguerite there and tried to persuade her son-in-law, Henry of Navarre, to visit her as well, but, not trusting her, Henry declined the invitation. In October 1548 she was at the château with Henry III when the plague broke out in Touraine. Two young women in her entourage, Mademoiselle de Montmorin and Mademoiselle de Rostaing, caught the contagion and died, and Catherine de' Medici and Queen Louise were obliged to flee. Catherine came again to the château in 1586 and 1587 to inspect the progress of the work. As the abbé Chevalier was to write three centuries later, Chenonceau was indeed a haven of peace. After mentioning the châteaux of Blois, Chaumont, Amboise, Loches, and Plessis-lès-Tours, the abbé added: "Chenonceau alone has no blood on its stones; in perfect harmony with the beautiful country surrounding it, it has never been mixed up in dismal political events; no groans were ever heard beneath its vaults; and all about it speaks to us exclusively of art and beauty, festivities and pleasures."[56]

[55] See Pierre de L'Estoile, *Registre-Journal du règne d'Henri III,* Madeleine Lazard and Gilbert Schrenck (eds.), Geneva: Droz, 1996, vol. II, pp. 104 and 113.
[56] C. Chevalier, *Le Château de Chenonceau,* 1869, p. 7, and *Histoire abrégée de Chenonceau,* 1879, p. V.

∧ Diane's parterre.

∧ Catherine's parterre and the Marques' Tower.

## The Queen Mother's Grand Design

A true Medici, the Queen Mother was a builder and it was to her that the great architectural "inventor" Jacques Androuet Du Cerceau naturally dedicated the two volumes of his *Les Plus Excellents Bastiments de France* (The Most Excellent Buildings of France), which appeared successively in 1576 and 1579.[57] As he intimates in his two prefaces, he was aware that Catherine would derive a good deal of enjoyment from his works. Several of the large drawings he made specially for her—the château of Saint-Maur, the Tuileries, and Chenonceau—are mentioned in this book. He knew that the Queen Mother contemplated transforming Chenonceau into a royal residence, which would mean erecting numerous additional buildings to house servants, courtiers, and visiting grandees, as well as spaces for the receptions and entertainments. There was already something of the grandeur of Versailles in her project. And as the fashion for palatial Italianate architecture was then at its zenith, the royal buildings would have to blend with particularly magnificent and astonishing shapes combining courtyards, colonnades, and exedras with sophisticated plans derived from religious architecture.

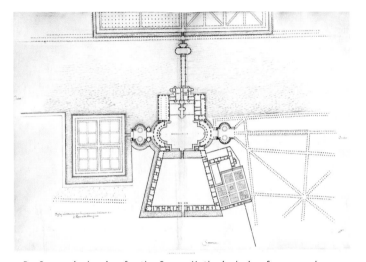

∧ Du Cerceau's drawing for the Queen Mother's design for a grander Chenonceau (LONDON, BRITISH MUSEUM), which differs in several respects from the plate in *Les Plus Excellents Bastiments de France*.

[57] For *Les Plus Excellents Bastiments de France* see the articles by Françoise Boudon, Hélène Couzy, and Gérard Rousset-Charny, *L'Information d'histoire de l'art,* 1974, n° 1, 2, and 3.

Her fabulous scheme for enlarging Chenonceau figures on one of the plates in
*Les Plus Excellents Bastiments*. It is entitled *"Augmentations de bastimens délibérés
faire par la Royne Mère du Roy"* (Building Extensions envisaged by the Queen Mother
of the King). The Bohiers' château and Diane's bridge were to be kept standing,
but were to be improved with the addition of a gallery and two flanking rectangular
constructions to be erected on the river and connected with the Terrace of
the Marques. The terrace itself was to be enlarged to colossal dimensions and
surrounded with colonnaded exedras. The old feudal tower was of course to be
sacrificed. A vast trapezoidal forecourt was to be laid out in front of the terrace.
The plan for the whole site was a huge triangle whose base lay along the entrance
wing of the forecourt and whose apex was an oval salon on the south end of the
bridge-gallery. This project was partly determined by some of Chenonceau's existing
features. Thus the oblique line of the service buildings abutting the pavilion garden
formed the right side of the trapezium. The left side may have been the abortive
project mentioned in 1552 for a gallery between the château and the garden
of Diane de Poitiers. Similarly, the Fontaine du Rocher, to which we will return later,
was probably one of a pair of motifs ornamenting the exedras on the right.

This ambitious design was perhaps stranger than that of the Tuileries, for it
reduced Chenonceau's original château to a mere focal point and gateway to the
covered bridge. As a utopian variation on the theme of a royal residence built on
water, it nevertheless reflected certain concrete decisions of Catherine de' Medici,
as Du Cerceau himself suggests: "The Queen Mother of the King being much pleased
with the situation, purchased the site and has since enlarged it with certain
buildings, intending to pursue [these improvements] in keeping with the design
which I traced on a plan." The project clearly had a connection with the Queen
Mother's letter patent of January 26, 1567, by which she makes her purpose known

∧ The Cher seen from one of the circular dormers
  above the gallery. Diane's parterre is on the left.

&gt; View of the Cher from the central dormer
  of the east façade of the château.

58 Anthony Blunt believed it was Du Cerceau, to whom he also attributed the grand design of the Tuileries. We have already mentioned the fact that in 1570 Catherine de' Medici still had in her possession several models that Philibert de l'Orme had made for her, but this does not prove that she used them seven years later.

59 Philibert de l'Orme, *L'Architecture,* Paris: Morel, 1567, Book III, figures pp. 66 and 67.

60 Strangely enough, none of these drawings is reproduced in W. H. Ward's invaluable *French Châteaux and Gardens in the XVIth Century. A series of reproductions of contemporary drawings hitherto unpublished by Jacques Androuet Du Cerceau,* London, 1909.

61 These drawings are reproduced in A. Blunt, *Philibert de l'Orme,* London: Zwemmer, 1958, fig. 38 a, reproduced here on p. 80.

62 Drawing of the plan of the contents of Chenonceau as it presently appears with the addition of the two gardens whose construction was deemed advisable (trans.). The plan is reproduced in

of "accommodating and embellishing" her estate and her decision to combine the revenues of Levroux with those of Chenonceau, "wishing to make expenditures greater than can be covered by the ordinary revenues of the said land and *seigneurie*." The project's author is still something of a mystery. After Philibert de l'Orme's death in 1570, Jean Bullant became the queen's architect. Bullant had been in the service of the Connétable de Montmorency before taking charge of the work site of Les Tuileries. Was he the man responsible for the scheme for enlarging Chenonceau, or was it Du Cerceau himself?[58] It is difficult to say, all the more so because the notion of including an existing edifice in an overall design in the modern manner, rather than remodeling it, is characteristic of de l'Orme.[59] Does this mean that the master plan for the greater Chenonceau was an idea Philibert suggested to Catherine, who then instructed Du Cerceau to flesh it out?

What is certain is that Du Cerceau came under the spell of Catherine's château. He devoted four of the engraved plates of the *Plus excellents bastiments* to it. Moreover, the British Museum owns five very rare drawings on vellum by Du Cerceau, showing notable differences from the engravings and apparently drawn on the site.[60] They were made long before the engravings, almost certainly between 1559 and 1565, after the transformation of the gardens and before the work on the château. One of the engravings is our only record of the plan of the expanded castle, and, as we have seen, it is not altogether reliable. The drawings of the upstream and downstream cross-sections of the château and bridge on a single sheet are both more accurate and more complete than the engravings.[61]

Moreover only the drawings—a bird's-eye view and a plan[62]—give us a view of the site as a whole. The parterres on the left bank are clearly visible on top, as are Diane's parterre south of the river, the green wood surrounding the Fontaine

K. Woodbridge, *Princely Gardens. The origin and development of the French formal style,* London: Thames and Hudson, 1986, p. 73. The bird's-eye view is reproduced in Blunt, *op. cit.*, fig. 39 a, and in J. Guillaume, "Le jardin mis en ordre," *Architecture, jardin, paysage...*, p. 131.

>

Du Cerceau, bird's-eye view of the château and grounds, *ca.* 1560-1565 *(Drawing Showing the Entire Contents of Chenonceau as it Presently Stands, with the Addition of Two Projected Gardens,* LONDON, BRITISH MUSEUM).

>

Plan by Du Cerceau, *ca.* 1560-1565 *(Drawing of the Plan of the Contents of Chenonceau as it Presently Stands with the Addition of the Two Gardens It Was Deemed Advisable to Establish,* LONDON, BRITISH MUSEUM).

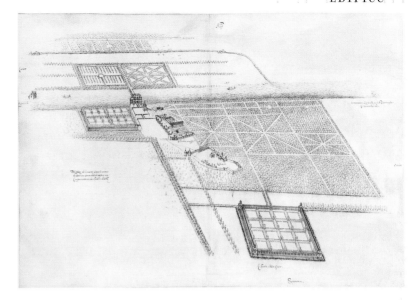

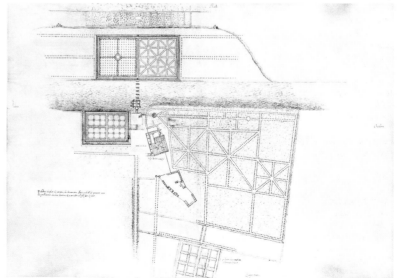

∧ The Marques' Tower. The château and the bridge-gallery from Catherine
de' Medici's parterre. The circular basin was built in 1984.

∧ The château viewed from the bridge and the sluice gate
controlling the level of the moat around Diane's parterre.

[63] In the far right-hand side of the bird's-eye view one can make out construction work beginning on a mill on a bridge, and on the far left hand-side a fortified mill built on the river.

[64] Reproduced in A. Blunt, *op. cit.*, fig. 39 b, reproduced here on p. 104. These differences concern mainly the layout of the ditches. The drawing shows the bridge's access on the south bank where it spans a canal running parallel to the river.

[65] See Le Plessis, *Les Triomphes, op. cit.* 1560.

[66] In a letter of Henry III, dated July 13, 1584, appointing him master builder at the château of Blois, Courtin is described as the architect for the Queen Mother's buildings at Chenonceau. In a letter dated October 4, 1586 (and not 1580, as C. Chevalier noted in his volume of 1868, p. 360) the Queen refers to Courtin having recently died. See *Lettres de Catherine de Médicis,* vol. IX, éditions Baguenault de Puchesse, 1905, p. 59.

[67] A letter of the Queen dated January 24, 1581, mentioned "the new buildings of a large gallery" at Chenonceau.

du Rocher, and the skewed alignment of the service buildings along the gardens of the pavilion, with the addition of a trellised gallery and a small pavilion at the intersection of the alleys. An entrance wing decorated with pilasters, of which only a single bay has been built, juts out at a sharp angle from the north-east corner of the service compound. Between it and the *basse cour* of the farm connected to the gateway between circular towers through which ran the original avenue to the castle, the words *"le jardrin accroisse"* (the expanded garden). The other garden project on the plan is a vast square parterre surrounded by galleries and ditches near the head of the avenue. Labeled *"le jardrin dont on est en délibération de faire"* (the garden under discussion), this garden was never built.[63] Of the grand design for Catherine's vision of a remodeled Chenonceau we thus have a drawn project, an engraving, and a number of very interesting differences between them.[64]

### Constructing the Gallery, Modernizing the Château

Chenonceau's bridge had been completed for Diane de Poitiers without a gallery or even a parapet, and so the Queen Mother's first move was to have gilt bronze balustrades erected along its sides. These are mentioned in the description of the entertainment of 1560.[65] Catherine's intention was to continue the work on the abortive project, but Chenonceau having become a royal residence financed with a much larger budget, a grander plan was now in order. A single gallery would not suffice for royal festivities, and so it was decided that even if this meant blocking the visual axis planned by the Bohiers the bridge would be covered with twin galleries built one on top of the other, crowned with an attic story large enough to sleep a throng of courtiers. The work began in 1576, at a time when the religious conflicts in the kingdom had been partly extinguished by the edict of Beaulieu-lès-Loches. Conducted by a master builder named Denis Courtin,[66] they were completed in 1581.[67]

\>

The north fireplace
in Catherine
de' Medici's lower
gallery. The
identical south
fireplace serves
merely as a
decorative frame
for the door to
the drawbridge.


\> \>

Following pages,
the lower
gallery with its
semicircular niches.

∧ The drawbridge to the
south bank.

∧ The south end of the gallery-
bridge showing the masonry
blocks once connecting it
to the former gate tower.

∧ Hercules, one of the herms
from the north façade.

[68] J. Guillaume also
compared it to the
decorative system Perino
del Vaga invented forty
years earlier on the walls
of the Sala Reggia at
the Vatican.

In a style quite unlike Philibert de l'Orme's subtle manner, Chenonceau's massive gallery was in all probability erected after Jean Bullant's drawings. Its Mannerist façades anticipate early seventeenth-century architecture. One is struck first of all by the semicircular ground-floor turrets resting heavily on the pointed buttresses of the piers. Inspired by the central motif Philibert de l'Orme had designed in 1557, they foreshadow the semicircular projections of the Pont-Neuf in Paris, conceived as a "balcony-bridge," the first stone of which was laid by Henry III on May 31, 1578.

At Chenonceau the turrets end in balconies along the first floor. The façades are more elaborate at this level than on the ground floor. Their tall windows are crowned with ample curved pediments. The base of these pediments is broken up by projecting jamb heads. Horizontal tables framed by moldings reminding one of interior paneling join the pediments together. This illusionist arrangement,[68] which masks the differences in the width of the piers while helping to frame the windows, has been compared to Jean Bullant's extremely graphic design for the Petit Château at Chantilly. Resting on a line of modillions, the cornice runs below a series of small stone dormers set back from the edge of the roof. The dormer windows are circular openings flanked by consoles and capped by decorated pediments in the manner of the new style instanced at the châteaux of Verneuil and Charleval.[69] Lastly, there are tall chimneys at both ends of the bridge roof. The alternating stone heads and consoles that top them were restored around 1870. On the interior the galleries form two superposed vessels almost 200 feet (60 m.) long and 19 feet (5.85 m.) wide ("18 *pieds*" in the estimate of 1557). Each gallery is flooded with light streaming in through eighteen windows. The lower gallery has eight absidioles fitted into the turrets. Tall decorated fireplaces stand at either end of both galleries. Pilasters ornamented with Catherine's monogram and carved heads represented full-face support the rampant arches of a broken pediment in the bottom gallery. The rampants in the top gallery are inverted above the chimney mantle and bear captives on one side and weapons trophies on the other. These are all reconstructions from the time of Madame Pelouze and her architect, Félix Roguet, based on remains of the south fireplace.[70] The French coat of arms on the north fireplace recall Henry II and his motto "*Hostibus intra ultraque devictis*." Opposite, on the south side, Catherine de' Medici's arms are figured with the device "*Litteris artibus ac rebus publicis*." As for the attic, it was furnished with a large number of sleeping quarters.

The gallery was to lead to a large oval salon on the river a few feet from the left bank, but in the end the builders chose not to demolish Diane de Poitiers' *châtelet*, perhaps for reasons of security. The protruding stones visible today over the unfinished southernmost bay are all that survive of this edifice. We do not know when it was destroyed; perhaps during the French Revolution.

[69] They were to be copied under the reign of Henry IV in the small gallery of the Louvre, as one can see on an engraving by Jean Marot.

[70] The sculptor, a native of Dijon, carved his name behind one of the captives: "Léon Breuil, 1876." The "fireplace of the captives" is shown on p. 207.

117

Not content with having twin galleries built on the bridge, Catherine decided to remodel the château itself. She wanted it expanded so as to be able to receive the large royal family there, and she wanted to replace its numerous Gothic features with more classical ornaments. For the festivities of 1560 the entrance façade was altered with the addition of two busts on the first-floor level of the central bay.

Moreover two windows were fitted into each of the flanking bays. In the narrow piers between the windows four sculpted herms were placed, representing Hercules, Pallas, Apollo, and Cybele, no doubt to recall the Pallas and the personification of Fame that had greeted King Francis II on this very spot. Of fairly mediocre workmanship, they were removed in 1866 by Félix Roguet and the façade was restored to its original appearance. The statues were reinstalled in the park near the maze.

Catherine also had the château's east façade altered. A two-story building was erected on the terrace between the chapel and the terrace. This increased the castle's box-like volume, but it reduced the light in the Salle des Gardes—hence the new openings on the entrance façade we have just mentioned.

∧ The château as altered by Catherine de' Medici. Woodcut by Andrew Best Leloir, 1855.

The new façade to the east now consisted of a pair of superposed projecting arcades below a broad triangular pediment flanked by two trophies. The lower arcade included a window imitating Lescot's ground-floor windows at the Louvre. A sacristy and a large bed-chamber were installed. The original arch supporting the terrace was enlarged and reinforced in the rustic manner fashionable at the time,

∧ Catherine de' Medici's alterations on the north façade. Mid-nineteenth-century engraving.

with massive voussoirs and a projecting keystone. Two centuries later, connoisseurs of architecture considered this structure poised on pier buttresses "a bold and skillful piece of masonry."[71] The building, which is visible on engravings and early photographs, was demolished in the course of Félix Roguet's renovation work.

The Queen Mother had the apartments decorated as well. Ceilings were painted, fireplaces built, interior walls covered with tapestries and gilt Cordoba leather, and windows were adorned with stained-glass.[72] In 1579 Georges Dubois, a glass painter from Tours, was commissioned to ornament the panes of the eighteen windows of the lower gallery with paintings after designs by the king's painter François Bunel.[73] Catherine de' Medici's apartment on the east side of the ground floor comprised the Salle des Gardes; a large bed-chamber—its sculpted fireplace and the monogram H C on the cornice are still there; the green cabinet furnished with hangings and armchairs upholstered in green velvet with black and white fringes, and its ceiling spangled with the monogram CC; and the library overlooking the Cher. We can form an idea of what Catherine's apartment must have looked like from the Cabinet des Grelots at the château de Beauregard.

To animate the niches of the lower gallery Catherine had classical statues imported from Italy. This is attested by two seventeenth-century accounts. "One sees there a quantity of ancient figures brought from Italy, which are said to be very rich, especially the figure of Scipio the African made of a certain

121

[71] Dupas de La Chauvinière, *Discours historique...*, 1745.
[72] *Notice sur les vitraux remarquables du cabinet de M. Vergnaud-Romagnesi, à Orléans, provenent du château de Chenonceau..., Orléans*, nd. (Chenonceau Archives, 11/90).
[73] See C. Chevalier, *Histoire abrégée de Chenonceau*, 1879, p. 219.

< The Cabinet Vert and
the door to the library.

∧ Thomas Bohier's Library.

stone that is ranked with valuable gems, and a quantity of other beautiful rarities worth beholding."[74] The niches, writes another visitor, are filled "with half-statues, busts of Roman emperors, which are of white marble, all of them modern, except for a bust of Scipio the African, in black marble, and one or two other busts in white marble from the Late Empire."[75] As for the white marble medallions (Galba, Claudius, Germanicus, Vitellius, and Nero) adorning the second-story corridor, they most likely date from the days of Thomas Bohier.

[74] Printed in Frankfurt in 1671, this account by a German traveler is given as an appendix in A. Galitzin's edition of Dupas de La Chauvinière.

∧ Catherine de' Medici's monogram on the ceiling of the Cabinet Vert.

∧ Fleur de lys on an ornamental tile.

∧ Monogram of Catherine de' Medici on the fireplace in her bed-chamber (nineteenth century).

[75] Voyage en France du sieur Du Buisson, with an introduction by A. Galitzin, *Mémoires de la Société archéologique de Touraine,* vol. XI, 1859, pp. 130-136.

### Catherine de' Medici's New Gardens

To flatter the queen, court poets deplored the fact that Diane de Poitiers had left Chenonceau in a woeful state. A sonnet of 1560 describes the gardens barren of flowers as "bushy deserts." So "displeased with the horror" of their "savage brambles" are the nymphs and gods that they have gone into hiding. Catherine needed little prompting on this subject: she had a passion for gardens and proved it the minute she acquired her residences at Montceaux, Saint-Maur, and especially the Tuileries in Paris, where she laid out parterres with the help of her

^ Antoine Caron, *The Young Charles IX Learning the Fine Arts in a Garden*. Cartoon for a tapestry, 1562 (PARIS, MUSÉE DU LOUVRE, CABINET DES DESSINS).

favorite, Marie de Pierrevive, the wife of the banker Antoine de Gondi.[76]

This backdrop of landscaped gardens brings us to the emblematic figure of Bernard Palissy. Imprisoned in Bordeaux as a result of Henry II's edict against heretics, Palissy wrote his first book on the proper way to use nature and its resources, *Recepte véritable par laquelle tous les hommes de la France pourront apprendre à multiplier leurs thrésors* (True Recipe by which all the Men of France May Learn to Multiply their Treasures).[77] Published at La Rochelle in 1563-1564 after Palissy's release, it featured the "design of a garden as delectable and of useful invention as was ever conceived." It was dedicated to the author's protectors, the Connétable de Montmorency and his son, and to the Queen Mother, to whom he declared: "There are things written in this book which could greatly assist in the setting up of your garden of Chenonceau; and when it pleases you to command me to be of service to you, I shall not fail to occupy myself there. And if such should be your wish, I shall do things that no one else has yet done up until now."

Historians have tried to determine the part Palissy played in designing the Queen Mother's new gardens.[78] It has been pointed out that although the flat, wooded site on the right bank simply did not conform to his ideal project which calls for the presence of a "mountain," the park of Francueil on the left bank lent itself admirably to laying out a garden in a gentle slope between the hillside, with its

125

76 See K. Woodbridge, *Princely Gardens, op. cit.*, chapter 5.
77 Bernard Palissy, *Œuvres complètes,* Paul-Antoine Cap (ed.), 1844. Recent editions by Jean Orcel (1961), Keith Cameron and Marie-Madeleine Fragonard (1996).
78 In his *Histoire abrégée de Chenonceau*, 1879, pp. 204-209, C. Chevalier categorically attributes the gardens on the right bank of the Cher, the Fontaine du Rocher, and the aviary to Palissy. See also Léonard N. Amico, *À la recherche du paradis terrestre. Bernard Palissy et ses continuateurs,* Paris: Flammarion, 1995.

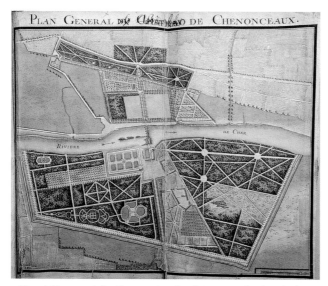

PLAN GENERAL DU CHATEAU DE CHENONCEAUX.

^ The château and its three parks. Hand-drawn and colored plan by Dupas de La Chauvinière, 1735 (CHENONCEAU ARCHIVES, VOL. 107).

128

caves and wine cellars and the banks of the Cher—the kind of garden the obstinate Hugenot described as a "true return to the Paradise of Genesis and the Psalms," a "garden of pleasance" surrounded by pastures watered by a stream (in this instance, the Vestin).

No written record of this collaboration survives, and a few tantalizing hints are all we have: a possible meeting between Palissy and Catherine at Saintes in 1565; the possibility, too, that Palissy may have left de Montmorency's service to work for the queen; and the fact that he was on good terms with the archbishop of Tours' grand vicar, the abbot of Turpenay, who was, as we have seen, one of the creators of the parterre of Diane. Thus Palissy may well have inspired, if not actually designed, the new gardens at Francueil, their low parterres separated by a central avenue leading to an amphitheater and the upper alley we see on Du Cerceau's drawings[79] and, even more clearly, on the Dupas de La Chauvinière hand-colored plan of 1735. The dates fit, since the garden was said to have been "recently set up" when the queen visited Chenonceau with Charles IX in 1565.[80] The wall enclosing the park to the south along the *route nationale* 76, was called the "*Mur de la Reine*" (Queen's Wall) in the abbé Chevalier's time.[81] Vestiges of the Fontaine d'Henri III are still to be seen there. The fountain's excellent water was specially reserved for the royal table,[82] another indication of Palissy's

[79] A canal running parallel to the Cher is even visible on the project for the grand design (reproduced p. 104).

[80] Description in a document drawn up in September 1565 for Catherine de' Medicis (Chenonceau archives, vol. 30).

[81] C. Chevalier, *Archives royales de Chenonceau*, vol. I, p. XIII.

[82] This fountain still feeds a basin of drinkable water.

possible influence, for the great ceramist was so keenly interested in "the nature of waters and fonts both natural and artificial," that he devoted the first chapter of his *Discours admirable* published in Paris in 1580 to this topic.

∧ Fountain enclosed by a trellised bower within a cave adorned with architectural elements. Engraving from the French edition of the *Hypnerotomachia Poliphili*, 1546.

Trellised bowers resting on 130 carved octagonal pilasters were added to the north and south sides of Diane's parterre and the queen had a pavilion erected at its entrance. The Pavillon de la Chancellerie, as it is called, was designed to house Catherine's pages and secretary, just as the Tour des Marques now became the lodging of the château's steward and keeper. Further west, close to the Cher, a "green garden" was laid out, inspired by the queen's beloved father-in-law Francis I's Jardin des Pins at Fontainebleau, with its plantations of evergreen trees and shrubs—pines, yews, boxwood, rosemary, laurels,

129

ilex—as well as olive, orange, and lemon trees in crates which were brought out in summer. It was designed by an Italian, Henri le Calabrese, and, after 1586, his assistant Jean Collo, or Jean Messine. A network of small fountains was built in the woods by the fountain master Picard Delphe or Delfi. Fragments of the conduits leading to five fountains arranged symmetrically in the compartments of the parterre were uncovered when Madame Pelouze's new gardens were dug in 1867.[83]

[83] C. Chevalier, *Histoire abrégée de Chenonceau*, *op. cit.*, p. 213; also in *Restauration de Chenonceau*, 1878.

The Pavillon
de la Chancellerie
from the château
forecourt.

[84] In 1563 Palissy published
a description of the
connétable's grotto.
This has fortunately been
found and reissued
(L. N. Amico, *op. cit.*).
Of the abundant
literature on Palissy's
grottos, Louis Dimier's
"Bernard Palissy
rocailleur, fontainier et
decorateur de jardins,"
*Gazette des Beaux-Arts,*
July 1934, pp. 8-29, is
particularly informative,
as are the various articles
on the Tuileries grotto
and the discovery of
the workshop where
its elements were made
during excavations of
the Louvre's foundations,
in *La Revue de l'art,*
no. 78, 1987.

At Catherine's bidding the Fontaine du Rocher, which had been built for Diane de Poitiers at the center of what was now the Jardin Vert, was transformed into a novel object that became the talk of the court: a grotto complete with artificial stalactites and terra-cotta figures of animals. In Du Cerceau's words, it was "a fountain within a Rock, [consisting] of several jets of water" cascading into a basin three *toises* (18 feet) in diameter. It was circled by a terraced alley and a second terrace, 8 to 10 feet higher, shaded by trellised vine-clad arbors enclosed by a wall adorned with columns, niches, statues, and stone benches. With its mound of rocks, the fountain represented Mount Parnassus in classical mythology, as did the Fontaine du Lydieu which was erected around the same time for Cardinal de Bourbon in the gardens of Gaillon. Palissy surely had a hand in the Chenonceau project: he had been working since 1555 on a grotto for the Connétable de Montmorency's gardens at Ecouen[84] and was soon to execute another grotto for the Queen Mother, this time in the gardens of the Tuileries. The new Fontaine du Rocher was not installed in time for the royal entertainment of 1563, but was in place for the festival of 1577.

Some distance from the fountain, in the area of the Pavillon, Catherine had an aviary built as well as a "menagerie" for sheep, Barbary goats, and a civet. The Queen Mother was also particularly interested in cultivating grape vines and in breeding silk worms. Silk worm hatcheries and a filature were installed in the former château of Les Houdes in 1582.

But the late sixteenth century was a violent age and the domain had to be protected as well. Work on a network of stone-lined moats or canals 39 feet (12 m.) wide and, on average, 16 feet (5 m.) deep was begun in 1584. This had been done twenty years earlier under Primaticcio's supervision in the middle

131

< The Pavillon de la Chancellerie viewed
  from Diane's parterre.

∧ The château and the avenue of linden trees
  skirting Les Dômes.

of the Cour du Cheval Blanc at Fontainebleau. In 1586 Jean François, the king's architect and master-mason in the Touraine, reported that the work on the canals of Chenonceau had been completed and was satisfactory.[85] Fed by two sluices on the Cher, the artificial waterways kept the land well drained and created a delightful water garden[86] that extended over a very large area. The canals bordered the main avenue, enclosed the parks, and provided a defense of the forecourt and terrace.

∧ The Wing of Les Dômes. Pencil and wash by Dupas de La Chauvinière, 1735 (CHENONCEAU ARCHIVES, VOL. 107).

[85] The contract for the work is dated October 1-4, 1584, Jean François' acceptance, August 23, 1586. See C. Chevalier, *Archives royales de Chenonceau*, vol. III, no. XXXIV.
[86] See Françoise Boudon, "Jardins d'eau et jardins de pente dans la France de la Renaissance," *Architecture, jardin, paysage...*, p. 141.

## The "Dômes"

With the construction of the gallery and the laying-out of a vast forecourt opposite the entrance avenue, as shown on Du Cerceau's drawings, the first stage of the grand scheme was well underway. The task of replacing the small service buildings on the west side of the base-court with an organized wing was the object of a final program of building. Designed to provide quarters for the Queen Mother's chaplain and her gentlemen-in-waiting, and to house the château's buttery and wine-cellar, the new building was remarkable for its dome-like roof, a reversed ship's hull imitating the outline of an imperial dome. De l'Orme had invented this type of wooden roof structure to avoid having to use very long timbers. He had experimented with it at the château de la Muette, the pall-mall court at Montceaux, and the ballroom at Limours. He recommended its construction in 1561 in his treatise *Nouvelles Inventions pour bien bastir et à petits fraiz* (New Inventions for Building Well and at Little Expense).[87] Called "Les Dômes" for obvious reasons, the building consists of a ground floor capped by stone dormers and rhythmically organized into three pavilions.

The construction of the wing of Les Dômes began after 1580 and was finished and accepted in August 1586.[88] Like the bridge-gallery, it was doubtless also the work of Denis Courtin, either after his own designs, those of Jean Bullant (who died in 1578), or those of Bullant's successor, Baptiste Androuet Du Cerceau. The north pavilion, or Pavillon de Fiesque as it was formerly called, shows traces of an older construction. Overall, the wing of Les Dômes has undergone alterations, making it difficult to say whether the fact that only three sides of the wing were completed means that the grand scheme was dropped after the work on the new wing shown on one of Du Cerceau's drawings was suspended. Its openings, its ornaments, and the shape of its attic (later reconstructed by Claude Dupin) were all modified when Félix Roguet converted it into stables in 1865. One gets an idea of its original appearance and lay-out from certain eighteenth-century views.[89] At the time the wing was part of an ensemble of buildings enclosing the aviary and the Jardins du Pavillon.[90] In Catherine's time the buildings of the old farm, which look like they are grouped around a village green, served as housing and workshops for the craftsmen working on Chenonceau's buildings, gardens, and fountains. Some of them were used as stables, for in keeping with a long-standing tradition stables had to be located as far as possible from a lord's manor.

Until 1586-1587, the indefatigable old queen made sure that the work on the property continued. One of the numerous graffiti on the upper level of one of the turrets states with almost symbolic force: *"L'on s'en va demain le 24 octobre* [We are leaving tomorrow 24 October] - *W Bertet, 1586."* The names of other

[87] Fol. 15 v°, 20 v°, 24 r°.

[88] The mason was Mathurin Hurlu. The timber framework of the roof was constructed by Denis Savare and the roof covering was by François Gourdet. Baptiste Du Cerceau, the son of Jacques (who died in early 1586), worked in Paris for Catherine de' Medici, who protected him even though he was a Huguenot. In a letter of December 23, 1856, she intimated that she still required one of the Du Cerceau brothers (either Baptiste or Jacques the Younger) at Chenonceau.

[89] An engraving by Dupin de Franceuil and a watercolor by La Chauvinière (1735).

[90] The nature and function of the buildings is listed in Queen Louise's *Inventaire* of 1604 which A. Galitzin published in 1856. The service premises included a dining hall for the late queen's retinue, kitchens, lodging for the head gardener, the fountain master, and the tailor. The "valet of furs" and the carpenter were housed in "the rear farmyard." The "menagerie" included quarters for a certain Mademoiselle de Glanderon.

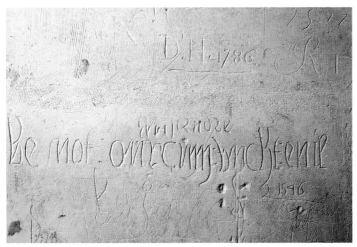

∧ Graffiti by Scottish guards on the chapel wall.

[91] An older inscription in the chapel deserves to be mentioned as well: *"Lavigne a faict grand déshonneur au roy auprès de Rostan, bassa et du grant seigneur, estant à Constantinople residant son ambassadeur, 1559"* (Lavigne did a great dishonor to the king in the court of Rostan, the [Turkish] *bassa* and great lord, when he was resident ambassador at Constantinople. 1559).

>

Les Dômes and the Chancellerie from Diane's parterre.

pages and maids-in-waiting surround it, with dates ranging between 1577 and 1586. Similar inscriptions refer to events in the daily life of the royal household. In the chapel, sentences in Old Scottish, signatures, and the dates 1543, 1546, and 1548 can be seen.[91] The dates 1586 and 1595 and the names Kunischaffer, Von Bremgarten, and J. Hans—presumably German foot soldiers—are carved in the stone walls of the Salle des Gardes.

Catherine counseled her beloved son and continued to have a hand in ruling the kingdom, but the increasing power of the League and the Guises complicated matters and prompted Henry III to take decisions on his own. The Day of the Barricades, the king's flight to Chartres, the dismissal of the king's men from the royal council, the convening of the States General at Blois and the killing of the Scarred One (Henry de Guise) and his brother Cardinal of Guise, all contributed to the Queen Mother's declining health and power. She took to her bed on the morrow of the crisis and, a few days later, on January 5, 1589, died at the age of 71. "She had hardly breathed her last breath," writes Pierre de L'Estoile, "than she was no more esteemed than a dead goat." In her will, the terms of which the king dictated to her on her death bed, she bequeathed Chenonceau to her daughter-in-law, Queen Louise.

# 5
# A Haven in a Troubled Age

Nimphes de Chenonceau, qui dans les ondes blues

De sa fontaine vive, habitez inconqneues

Ce Parnasse françois, et reflétant vos yeux

Du cristal azuré qui r'ouvre les cieulx,

Frisez vos tresses d'or, où Zéphyre se joue.

Nymphs of Chenonceau, who in the blue water

Of its gushing font secretly inhabit

That French Parnassus, your eyes reflecting

The azure crystal that sweeps the skies clear again,

Curl your golden tresses where Zephyr plays.

Du Perron, *Estreynes au Roy* (Henri III),
probably alluding to the Fontaine Henri III

## Queen Louise in Mourning

The era of Chenonceau's builders, especially the great women who shaped it, had come to an end. By 1559 the château stood virtually as we see it today. This does not mean, however, that it ceased to play a part in France's history.

∧ Jean Rabel, *Queen Louise of Lorraine,* *ca*. 1575. Color pencil drawing (BIBLIOTHÈQUE NATIONALE DE FRANCE, CABINET DES ESTAMPES).

Henry III's wife Louise de Lorraine-Vaudémont has a place of her own in the portrait gallery of France's queens. Her marriage to the monarch was a love match and till the day of her death she remained loyal to the memory of her husband, a ruler history has not been kind to. The daughter of one of the younger princes of the house of Lorraine, she caught the eye of Henry III in 1573 when the French king stopped in Nancy on his way to Cracow to be crowned King of Poland. After returning to France he decided to yield to his inclination for her and announced that he was going to marry "a woman of his nation who was agreeable and beautiful" adding that, "desiring one he could cherish and have children with," he did not intend to seek a wife far abroad as his predecessors had done.[92] Though she dreamt of a more brilliant match for her son, the Queen Mother felt that the mild-mannered and pious Louise would not interfere with the business of the realm. Not only did she not oppose Henry's choice, she magnanimously included Louise in all court ceremonies. The wedding was held in Rheims two years later, following Henry's coronation . Henry III was certainly not a faithful husband—his escapades were numerous and his liaison with Mademoiselle

[92] Cited in Madeleine Lazard, *Les Avenues de Fémynie,* Paris: Fayard, 2001, p. 356.

de Châteauneuf long-standing—but Louise turned a deaf ear to court rumors
and the king was genuinely fond of her. In 1582 he resolved to reform his ways
and thereafter the royal pair were more closely united in their forever disappointed
hope of having children. Though related to the Guises, Louise was a loyal supporter
of her husband's policies and stood by his side during the crisis of 1588.

∧ ∧ Symbols of Queen Louise's bereavement in her bed-chamber.

When, a year later, Henry III was assassinated by Jacques Clément during the
siege of Paris, 36-year-old Louise, who had stayed behind in the Touraine,
was disconsolate. The king, still uncertain of the outcome of his wound, wrote
to her from his bed at Saint-Cloud, "My sweet, I hope to be perfectly well;
pray God for me and don't move from where you are." After his death, Louise
gradually distanced herself from the partisans of the League in her family and
eventually gave her far-from-negligible support to Henry IV even before the new

143

∧ Diane's parterre.

∧ The château viewed from Diane's parterre.

king, a Protestant, converted to Catholicism. Henry's separation from Marguerite of Valois left Louise the sole queen of France until Marie de' Medici arrived on the scene in 1601. Known from then on as the "White Queen," white being the color of mourning for queens, Louise made Chenonceau her hermitage.

After inheriting the property from Catherine, Louise had received the court here in the days when Henry III was still alive and had temporarily established his capital in Tours. And it was here, in the château, that she got the news of his death. She chose as her private chamber the new room built on the terrace, for it adjoined the chapel. Through a bull's-eye window and an opening in the sacristy wall she was able when tired to follow mass from her own bed. She spent her days praying, reading, and doing needlework amid furnishings that reminded her constantly of her bereavement. The walls and ceiling of her chamber and the oratory were painted black[93] and adorned with silver tears, feathers, bones, and gravediggers' implements. This pattern was repeated on the furniture upholstery, the drapes, the curtains of her bed, and on silk and velvet taffeta wall hangings which were brought out on feast days. On the mantelpiece hung a painting depicting Catherine de' Medici flanked by Henry III and Louise, with the motto "*Vivite felices quibus est fortuna peracta*" (Live happily, you whose destiny has been accomplished). The mantelpiece in the neighboring Green Cabinet displayed a portrait of the late king and its inscription, taken from Virgil, read: "*Saevi monumenta doloris*" (testimonies of a cruel sorrow). In this setting the Dowager Queen spent eleven years in bereavement, surrounded by a small retinue of followers led by her *chevalier d'honneur*, the Comte de Fiesque, and his wife, Alphonsine Strozzi, who were housed in the Pavillon des Marques. Louise only left the château on Saturdays, to attend a regular weekly mass for her husband in the parish church of Francueil.

<
Reconstruction on the second story of Queen Louise's ground-floor bed-chamber, with the original ceiling.

[93] The abbé Chevalier describes seeing Queen Louise's chamber in the original state. The room was dismantled during the restoration work conducted by F. Roguet in 1866, but the décor has been recently reconstructed in a room on the château's second floor.

∧ The "Francis I bed-chamber."

∧ The "Gabrielle d'Estrées bed-chamber."

France was still not pacified. In the winter of 1589-1590, there was fighting close to Chenonceau. Partisans of the League captured the stronghold of Montrichard. Henry IV, temporarily based in Tours, despatched Sully to retake the town. Bivouacking on Chenonceau's lands, the royal troops caused "a thousand ravages" and Louise requested Henry to order them to leave. Nor was this her only message to the king: she repeatedly pressed him to have Jacques Clément's accomplices hunted down and brought to trial. In January 1594 she even traveled to his camp at Mantes to complain that the dower she was entitled to as a royal widow had still not been transferred to her and that her income was insufficient to live on. In July 1592 she energetically petitioned the Parliament to rescue her from "the poverty" in which she lived. The revenues from her *châtellenie* being all she had, the king decided to grant her a modest pension of 12,000 *écus* from his personal treasury.

[94] C. Chevalier, *Archives royales de Chenonceau*, vol. IV (debts and creditors of Catherine de' Medici), 1862.

Louise was obliged to deal with her mother-in-law's creditors, for on her death Catherine had left debts totaling 800,000 *écus*.[94] Well aware of his mother's extravagant habits, Henry III had had Chenonceau declared unforfeitable property on the specious grounds that his mother had "taken to heart and delighted in" embellishing it more than any other place and that it had to remain at the disposal of his "dear companion," the queen, in memory of the Queen Mother who had loved her so dearly. But these fine sentiments cut little weight with Catherine's creditors and, as almost all the properties of the late queen had been usurped in the course of the civil wars, they succeeded, on December 5, 1597, in getting Parliament to rule that Queen Louise had either to pay Catherine's debts and the estate's running expenses or pack up. At this point another woman intervened, the new royal mistress, Gabrielle d'Estrées, Duchess of Beaufort. Hoping to acquire Chenonceau for herself, this veritable reincarnation of Diane de Poitiers promptly bought up the creditors' rights for 22,000 *écus*. The realm's legal machinery ground away through the following year, unmoved by the feelings of the White Queen, who was spared no humiliation: Chenonceau was sequestered, bills were posted, a first auction was held.

∧ Ambroise Dubois, allegorical portrait of Gabrielle d'Estrées as Diana the Huntress (CHÂTEAU DE CHENONCEAU).

The château was again saved through political maneuvering. Queen Louise's brother, Philippe-Emmanuel de Lorraine, Duke of Mercœur, was the governor of Brittany and the last leading League partisan to hold out against the crown. Henry IV was concluding the Edict of Nantes, which he hoped would put an end to the religious strife in the realm, and concurrently carrying on negotiations toward a settlement with the duke. Pursuing this goal, he came to Chenonceau in February 1598. His mistress Gabrielle had thought of a solution: her young son César, fathered by the king, would be betrothed to the duke's only daughter, Françoise. Through her mother, Marie of Luxembourg, Françoise stood to inherit the immense fortune of the House of Penthièvre. Queen Louise took an active role in bringing the negotiations to a successful conclusion and to secure a reconciliation between the duke and the crown—and thus the complete pacification of France.

After all the details were settled, Henry, Gabrielle, and the Mercœurs came to Chenonceau to pay a visit to the queen to whom they owed so much.

151

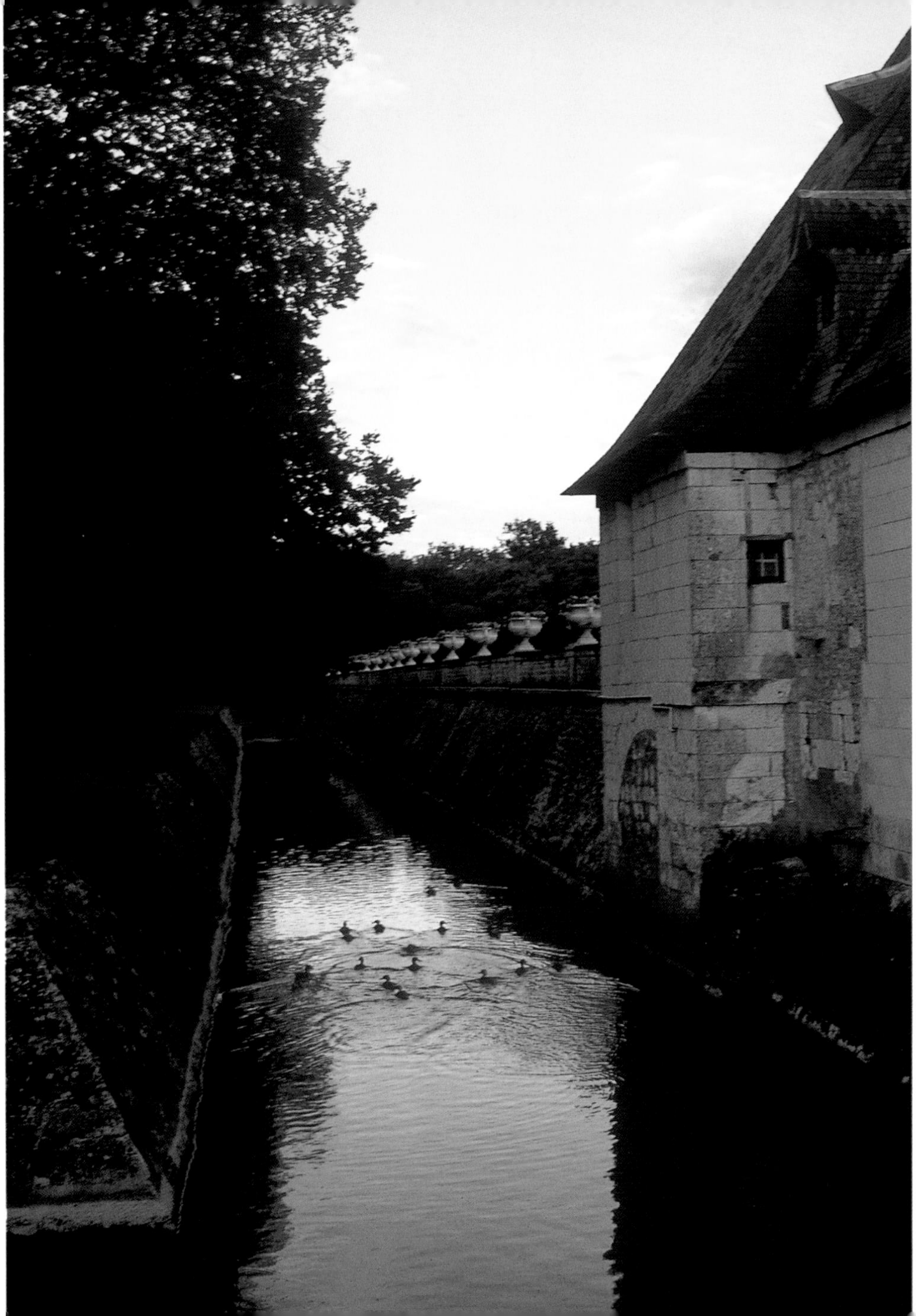

‹ The moat on the north side of Diane's parterre.

∧ The château from the northeast.

Louise then announced that she would make a gift of the château to the betrothed on condition that Gabrielle forego the rights she had acquired from the Queen Mother's creditors. To this the king's favorite promptly agreed. The Duke of Mercœur guaranteed Louise's liability and the deed of donation was signed on October 15, 1598. However the troubles of Louise, who had retained the right to continue living at Chenonceau, were not at an end. She was obliged to sell some of her pearls to pay back Catherine's creditors and had to receive the Parliament's comptrollers sent to assess the state of dereliction of the castle and the tenant farms, which had been neglected for a decade. Meanwhile Louise was at last given her dower, the province of the Bourbonnais, previously in the hands of Charles IX's widow, Elisabeth of Austria. She was on her way to take formal possession of it when she died in Moulins on January 29, 1601.[95]

Queen Louise, like Henry III, had taken an interest in introducing into France the Capuchin order, a branch that had recently broken away from the Franciscans. She had even planned to retire to a Capuchin nunnery and had left 20,000 *écus* for a convent to be built at Bourges, where she wished to be buried. After her death, the Duchess of Mercœur had the foundation transferred to the Faubourg Saint-Honoré in Paris and, with the approval of the pope and the king, a Capuchin convent was built there in 1604. Three years later it became Louise's final resting place.

### The Duchess of Mercœur

On February 20, 1601, Henry IV sent César Forget, *sieur* de Baudry, to take formal possession of the château in the name of his son César, Duke of Vendôme. But fate had decreed that the title to Chenonceau was never to be transferred smoothly. Queen Catherine's creditors proved unwilling to renounce the estate's revenues, and as a result the Duchess of Mercœur, widowed in 1602, offered to acquire the land

[95] A. Galitzin (ed.), *Inventaire des meubles, bijoux et livres estans à Chenonceau le huit janvier M.DC.III,* Paris: Téchener, 1856.

∧ Assembly room for the Capuchin nuns
in the château's attic.

∧ The interior drawbridge leading
to the conventual quarters.

herself for 96,300 *livres*. The legal proceedings dragged on from 1602 to 1606, and in the end the duchess had to let go of all of the château's moveable furnishings, except the ancient statues. She had to pay personally for the maintenance of the fountains, the walls and roofs of the tenant farms, and the drawbridge on the left bank. At her own expense, the wooden bridge between the Marques' Tower and the Fontaine du Rocher was replaced with a twin-arched stone bridge.[96]

96 This stone stairway bridge is clearly visible on one of Vairon's two lithographs of 1841 reproduced in *Notice historique sur le château de Chenonceau,* Tours: Mame, n.d.

Madame de Mercœur was in no hurry to honor the promise to see her daughter united with the king's bastard son, whom she considered an unworthy match, but she had no real say in the matter and the wedding took place at Fontainebleau in July 1609. Then, only a year later, the assassination of Henry IV utterly

< The bridge between the forecourt and the terrace.

∧ ∨ Ornamental vases surrounding Diane's parterre.

changed France's political scene. César of Vendôme joined the coalition of princes disgruntled by Marie de' Medici and her favorite, Concini, and withdrew to Brittany, his domain. His mother-in-law retired from Court and, in 1611, settled in Chenonceau with her own mother, the Princess of Martigues. She devoted the last twelve years of her life there to political intrigues and prayer.

Out of piety she had sent for a small community of twelve Capuchin nuns, wanting to establish them in Tours. But the authorities there were reluctant to grant their approval and she put them up in the château, where they remained until 1634, when they finally received permission to settle in Tours. Conventual quarters were set up in the attic rooms formerly occupied by pages and maidens-in-waiting. There were cells, a refectory, an assembly room, and even a small oratory above the chapel vault. A passageway was built between the convent and the chambers of the duchess, who had moved into Queen Louise's apartment. The nuns were protected from the outside world by a drawbridge operated from above at the other end of the château. These arrangements were long a source of wonder to visitors, and some of them, notably the drawbridge, still survive.[97]

The Court continued to bear a grudge against the duchess and made this cruelly clear on July 19, 1614, when the young Louis XIII rode scornfully past the gate of Chenonceau without stopping, on his way to Brittany where he was to preside over the States General and receive the submission of his brother César. However, a year later passions had cooled. On his name day, August 25, 1615, the king, traveling to Bordeaux to meet his betrothed, Anne of Austria, finally deigned to stop at the château. He "dined and spent the night at Chenonceau," wrote the physician Héroard, and watched "fireworks on the river, and on the morrow played at rings in the garden." The king and the court returned to the Touraine several

[97] The bridge was destroyed by Dupin in 1734, but was re-erected by Madame Pelouze.

times, but paid only one visit to the duchess. On August 9, 1619, Louis XIII showed the castle and the gardens to Queen Anne. The duchess spent her remaining years at Chenonceau, adding to it the estate of Civray which she had inherited from her mother. But it was in Anet that she died at the age of 63 on September 6, 1623. She was buried at the Capuchin convent in Paris, next to the White Queen.

### The Vendômes

Thereafter the Loire Valley ceased to be the haunt of royalty. It became a retreat or a land of exile, as the center of royal power became permanently established in and around Paris. For César de Vendôme and his wife, who inherited the duchess's vast holdings, Chenonceau was merely one of many estates, suitable at best for organizing an intrigue or nursing a grievance. A hardened plotter, Vendôme skulked in Chenonceau in 1624, the year Richelieu was admitted to the King's Council, and occupied himself restoring the gardens of Diane and Catherine to their original glory. After spending four years in prison at Amboise and Vincennes, he returned to the banks of the Cher in 1632-1633 and rebuilt in stone the bridge leading to the Marques' Terrace. Later he went into voluntary exile in the Lowlands and, later still, he moved to England.

His second son, the Duke of Beaufort, followed the same path. In 1637, the "King of the Halles," as he was known at the height of the Fronde, received his fellow conspirator, the King's brother Gaston of Orléans. Gaston had ridden over to Chenonceau on a "neighborly visit" from Blois, where he was building on a vast scale. In her *Memoirs*, the Grande Mademoiselle, who accompanied her father, left an awed account of their dinner at the château: "Eight courses of twelve dishes each, and so well served that not even in Paris would it have been possible to make it better or more magnificent." The princess found the manor

∧ The main avenue.

> Les Dômes from the back.

house to be "of the most extraordinary shape it is possible to see," but admired the gardens. She deplored the bareness of the two galleries: "All this house needs is a master willing to pay for the expense of painting and gilding."[98]

César de Vendôme thought that with the death of the much-hated Cardinal Richelieu in 1642, soon followed by that of the king, the power of the realm would at last be placed in the hands of an oligarchy. But he had not reckoned on the arrival of another man in scarlet, Cardinal Mazarin, nor on the regent, Queen Anne's, unwavering support of the Italian prelate. Having compromised himself in the Cabal of the Important Ones, the Bastard of the Béarnais eventually decided to submit and, in what must have been a final humiliation for him, negotiated the marriage of his older son, Louis de Mercœur, to one of the cardinal's nieces, Laure-Victoire Mancini. The reconciliation was sealed at Chenonceau on July 14, 1650, in the presence of the king, the Queen Mother, and Mazarin, during an elaborate court entertainment. This event, the last royal visit to Chenonceau, inspired the following description of the château in the doggerel of the *gazetier* Loret's *Voyage de la Cour à Chambord:*

> *Basti si magnifiquement, / Il est debout comme un géant / Dedans le lit de la rivière, / C'est-à-dire dessus un pont / Qui porte cent toises de long.*[99]

The young Mercœur and his wife were married in Paris on February 4, 1651. Chenonceau was their wedding gift. However the château bears little trace of their memory. Widowed four years later, Louis made a career in the Church and became a cardinal before dying in 1669. His two sons, Louis-Joseph, Duke of Vendôme, and the Chevalier Philippe, were initially placed in the care of a council of guardians who kept up Chenonceau, re-established the gardens in 1670, planted flowers and boxwood hedges in the Grand Parterre, and laid out

[98] This description can be rounded out with that of A. Félibien, *Mémoires pour servir à l'histoire des Maisons royalles et bastiments de France* (1684), A. de Montaiglon (ed.), Paris: Société de l'histoire de l'art français, 1874.
[99] "Built so splendidly,/ It stands like a giant/ In the bed of the river,/ That is to say on a bridge/Spanning a hundred *toises*" (trans.).

∧ Francis I's salamander on the fireplace of the royal bed-chamber. A nineteenth-century copy of an original carving at Blois.

∧ H. Rigaud, *Louis XIV*, 1701, given by the king to the duke of Vendôme.

163

100 Daniel Leloup, *Le Château d'Anet,* Paris: Belin-Herscher, 2001.

the Jardin de la Volière and the Jardin de Francueil. But on coming into their estate the two youths gave themselves over to such debauchery and dissipation that their property was sequestered and for the next two decades was administered by financial officers appointed by their creditors. Only when the duke began to reveal his brilliant military capacities at the head of the royal troops during the Spanish Wars of Succession, between 1695 and 1697, was he able to put an end to this humiliating arrangement, pay off his debts, and control the management of his estates. However, he preferred the château of Anet, which lay closer to Versailles and where he had undertaken substantial construction work as early as 1678.[100] He thus decided to mortgage Chenonceau for a life annuity

>
The royal
bed-chamber
successively
occupied by
Louis XIII and
Louis XIV. Like the
portrait by Lepautre
in its elaborate
frame, the gilt
chairs are thought
to have been a gift
of the king to
his cousin.

101 J.-P. Babelon, *Album du Comte du Nord. Recueil des plans de Chantilly en 1784*, Paris: Éditions M. Hayot, 2002, p. 58.

to François d'Illiers, otherwise known as the Chevalier d'Aulnay. Many of the château's remaining art works vanished, many of its statues were transferred to Anet, perhaps even to Versailles in an effort to curry the king's favor.

Yet it was to Chenonceau that Vendôme came to recuperate after the failure of the Flanders campaign and his temporary disgrace, and there it was that the worn-out, disfigured, 56 year-old bachelor took it into his head to get married. Mademoiselle d'Enghien, the 33-year-old granddaughter of the Grand Condé, let herself be persuaded. It is true that in the marriage contract they signed at Marly on May 13, 1710, the duke bequeathed all his property to her. These were the twilight years of the great reign of Louis XIV. Gone to Spain to defend the crown of Philip V, Vendôme died of indigestion on June 10, 1712, followed six years later by his wife, a victim, says Saint-Simon, of her immoderate fondness for strong spirits.

Chenonceau passed into the hands of the duke's mother, Anne of Bavaria, Dowager Princess of Condé and a princess palatine, who sold it to her grandson Louis Henry, Duke of Bourbon, Prince of Condé, minister to Louis XV and lord of the château of Chantilly. Louis Henry visited Chenonceau only once, in 1733, on his way back from the abbey of Beaumont-lès-Tours where he had accompanied his mother and his sister, who had been named abbess there. But, being a good manager, he invested 32,000 *livres* in repairing the château and its out-buildings and, judging from the fact that some of the parterres on La Chauvinière's plan of 1735 are almost identical to those his gardener Nicolas Breteuil laid out in Chantilly's Petit Parc,[101] he seems to have taken an interest in the gardens. But in truth he had no use for Chenonceau and on June 9, 1733, he sold it to a farmer general named Claude Dupin. The 130,000 *livres* he got from the sale financed about half of his purchase of the Duchy of Guise.

# 6
## MADAME DUPIN'S REALM

Qu'à m'égarer dans ces bocages

Mon cœur goûte de voluptés!

Que je me plais sous ces ombrages!

Que j'aime ces flots argentés!

Douce et charmante rêverie,

Solitude aimable et chérie,

Puissiez-vous toujours me charmer!

My heart delights in such pleasures

As I lose my way amid the hedges and trees!

How delightful these shady nooks!

How I love these silvery ripples!

Sweet, enchanting reverie,

Lovely and beloved solitude,

May you always captivate me!

Jean-Jacques Rousseau, *L'Allée de Sylvie*

The era of queens, duchesses, and royal mistresses was over. The Age of Enlightenment was among other things an age of great financiers, and a new society moved into France's aristocratic homes and enjoyed life there free from the stiffness of court etiquette. In a return to the days of the Bohiers, an ennobled financier became the new master of Chenonceau. The son of a Châteauroux tax receiver, Claude Dupin studied at the *collège* of Blois and began his career as an obscure local tax official. But his fortunes changed when he met the immensely wealthy banker of the court, Samuel Bernard. Thanks to Bernard's influence, he was appointed general receiver of finances of Metz and Alsace, and then, in 1726, he became one of France's forty *fermiers generaux* responsible for collecting the kingdom's taxes. At last he was in a position to exercise his brilliant mind and technical expertise and to impress the realm with his professionalism.[102] Meanwhile, in 1772, he had married his protector's fifteen-year-old bastard daughter, Louise-Marie-Madeleine Fontaine.

^ Jean-Marc Nattier, *Portrait of Madame Dupin,* *ca.* 1745 (CHÂTEAU DE CHENONCEAU). The sitter's mother was the Comédie Française actress Manon Dancourt.

102 Julie Ladant, "Le fermier général Claude Dupin," *Positions des thèses de l'École des chartes,* 2000, pp. 181-187.

His fund of knowledge in the economic field propelled him into the circles of the *philosophes* and the *Encyclopédie*. Diderot and D'Alembert asked him to assist them in their great enterprise. He took up his pen to write the three volumes of his great treatise, *Œconomiques,* issued in 1745. He even wrote a constructive criticism of Montesquieu's *L'Esprit des lois,* published in 1748, and in the Parisian society the Dupins frequented, the ensuing controversy was much talked about. Later, Claude purchased a position as secretary to the king, which carried a noble title, and, from 1732 to 1739, lived in the splendid Hôtel Lambert on the Île Saint-Louis in Paris. His wife was the hostess of one of the capital's most well-attended salons. Here the aristocracy mingled with the realm's richest men and its best minds—Fontanelle, the Abbé de Saint-Pierre, Voltaire, Marivaux, and Madame du Deffand and others.

Nothing was too costly or beautiful for the Dupins. The acquisition of Chenonceau in 1733 crowned their remarkable social ascension. Perhaps this was most concretely expressed in Claude Dupin's declaration of the buildings and grounds belonging to the estate in 1742. After mentioning the château, the proud new owner went on to list "My tower, *donjon* and fortress standing in the court of the said château, which court is enclosed by moats of flowing water."[103] Deeply attached to the estate, Dupin spent 70,000 *livres* improving it: he purchased several small fiefs bordering it, had the moats repaired, planted elms along the main avenue, lavished care on the domain's vineyards, and even hired a wine grower from Champagne to introduce *champenois* grapes and wine-growing methods. In 1740 plantations of white mulberries were established on the slopes at Francueil. The château's gardens, like the Jardin de la Volière behind the Domes (the roofs of which were remodeled), were redone in the style of the day, and the fountains in Diane and Catherine's parterres were removed. Inside the castle the Dupins, who had acquired the furniture from the former occupant, the Chevalier d'Aulnay, decorated and furnished the apartments in the latest manner and hung paintings by Old Masters. They did away with Queen Louise's funereal décor and with the conventual arrangements in the attic (1734), and divided the upper gallery into suites.

[103] Claude Dupin took a great interest in Chenonceau's history and charged the Abbé Gerbault with the task of putting the château's archives in order in 1738. The estate's receiver, Dupas de La Chauvinière, carried on this task from 1744 to 1748. In 1745 he completed for his master the first *Discours historique* on Chenonceau, which Prince Galitzin published in 1857. To La Chauvinière we are also indebted for several precious watercolors painted in 1735 (Chenonceau archives, vol. 107).

171

104 Extracts and various notes in Rousseau and Madame Dupin's handwriting were still in the archives at Chenonceau in Abbé Chevalier's day. These documents were later dispersed. Some of them, thanks to a gift by Marcel Dehaynin to the Institut de France, wound up at the Abbey of Chaalis.

Perhaps the best illustration of their years of residence in the Touraine is a little-known literary anecdote. Jean-Jacques Rousseau, who had arrived in Paris in 1741 with little to recommend him except a new system of musical notation, was introduced to Madame Dupin. She engaged him for a week to tutor her son Dupin de Chenonceau until the youth's regular tutor returned. The boy was a wastrel and, despite his youth, ran up such sizable gambling debts that his parents were obliged to sell their town house in Paris. "I spent those eight days in a torment which only the pleasure of obeying Madame Dupin made tolerable," writes the unfortunate Rousseau in his *Confessions*. Before long the Swiss-born philosopher found regular employment in the family's service as a secretary—or rather a literary assistant—to the mistress of the house. While Claude Dupin continued to write on political economy, his wife took a notion to writing about the virtues of women. On Rousseau's return to France from Venice in 1746, she asked him to edit her manuscript. The subject was of a nature to kindle his imagination, for in his youth he himself had considered writing on the same topic. Throwing himself enthusiastically into the project, he worked on it both in Paris and at Chenonceau. The book, however, never appeared in print.[104] Rousseau was also at the time laying the foundations of his treatise on education, *Émile*. When he confided to Madame Dupin his plan of giving up his illegitimate child with Thérèse Levasseur to an orphanage, she vainly tried to talk him out of it.

The philosopher spent the fall of 1747 at Chenonceau and left a detailed description of his sojourn there: "We enjoyed ourselves a great deal in that lovely place; the food was very good and I got fat as a monk." Madame Dupin liked to invite to her country estate the celebrities who frequented her salon in Paris—particularly Lord Bolingbroke, who had retired to nearby Chanteloup. The guests passed their time taking walks, reciting poetry, putting on plays, and listening

> View of the château
from the north
bank, drawn and
engraved by Dupin
de Francueil, and
dated April 14,
1739 (CHENONCEAU
ARCHIVES, VOL. 107).
The gate tower on
the south side of
the bridge-gallery
was still standing
at this time.

> The château seen
from the south
bank. Drawing by
Dupin de Francueil
and engraved by
Pierre Aveline,
*ca.* 1735 (CHENONCEAU
ARCHIVES, VOL. 107).

∧ ∨ > Chenonceau's vegetable garden.

to music. Thanks to his musical skills Rousseau became friendly with Louis-Claude Dupin de Francueil, the master of the house's son by a previous marriage. Keenly interested in chemistry and the physical sciences, Louis-Claude was also an accomplished violinist and a skilled lute-maker.[105] Rousseau composed trios to be sung by the Dupins and their set, and at Madame Dupin's request wrote a comedy, *L'Engagement téméraire,* in fifteen days. It was performed in a little theater at the end of the upper gallery. Rousseau was fond of strolling in the park, especially down one alley by the Cher, to which he gave its present name, *l'allée de Sylvie.* It still leads past a tree said to be "Jean-Jacques' oak."

Claude Dupin died in 1769, shortly after the death of his second son, Dupin de Chenonceau, whose wife had delighted Rousseau. As for Dupin de Francueil, like his father, he married twice. Widowed from his first wife, Madeleine Suzanne, with whom he had a daughter, he married the illegitimate daughter of the Maréchal de Saxe. Their son was George Sand's father.

Then, in 1770, Chenonceau nearly changed hands again. The wealthy minister Étienne-François Choiseul, who had been made duke and peer of Amboise, was especially fond of the nearby estate of Chanteloup, which he had acquired in 1761 and to which, following a political reversal, he was forced to retire in 1770. Wanting to annex the woods of Chenonceau to his domain he offered to buy the château's grounds; however, the deal came to nothing. Madame Dupin came often to the Touraine from Paris and devoted herself to charitable works for the poor of the estate's four parishes. She provided them with clothing and when they fell ill had them attended by a local physician named Bretonneau, whose son she helped through medical school. This was the illustrious Pierre Bretonneau (1778-1862), famous for his pioneering work on typhoid and diphtheria.

[105] He was also a skilled draftsman, and has left the two views of Chenonceau reproduced p. 175. One is dated April 14, 1739, and is engraved by him; the other was engraved by M. P. Aveline.

∧ Madame Dupin's tomb in the Parc de Francueil.

When the French Revolution broke out she left her home on the rue de la Plâtrière (now rue Jean-Jacques Rousseau) in Paris and took refuge at Chenonceau. So universally respected was she that the local revolutionaries left her alone. Having lost her grandson Dupin de Rochefort, for whose education Rousseau had written *Emile,* and her only nephew, Vallet de Villeneuve, the treasurer general of the City of Paris' domains, she

179

was an old and lonely woman. There was talk, to be sure, of seizing the château as national property "mortgaged by the tyrants of France," but Madame Dupin's legal representatives were able to prove that it had always been privately held. The revolutionary committee at Amboise even moved to have the château torn down, but the curate of Chenonceau, the abbé Lecomte persuaded them to leave it standing, as it was the only bridge across the Cher between Montrichard and Bléré. The abbé also managed to save most of the castle's archives from destruction.[106]

The *citoyenne* Dupin contributed generously to patriotic funds, loaned décor from the château to the theater at Loches, donated the estate's cannons to the city of Tours—and died in the last weeks of the eighteenth century, on November 20, 1799, at the age of 92. Her great-nephews arranged for her to be buried in the spot she had chosen, in a glen in the Parc de Francueil. Her grave[107] keeps alive the memory of a generous, witty woman.

[106] The abbé Lecomte kept up his ties with Chenonceau in the nineteenth century and wrote a history of the estate for the Countess of Villeneuve. In it he paid homage to the memory of Madame Dupin.

[107] The work of the architect Boynard and the sculptor Monpelier, Madame Dupin's tomb recalls Rousseau's famous island grave at Ermenonville.

∧ Sixteenth-century building
on Chenonceau's La Grange farm.

> Chenonceau's vineyards have produced
an excellent quality wine ever since
the Middle Ages.

# 7

# BACK TO THE French Renaissance

## TWO CENTURIES OF RESTORATION

*Praise to the one God!*

*I have seen the world gather in this château.*

*It is like a portion of the eternal garden.*

*Greetings to all who read what I have written.*

*I am Abd el-Kader ben Mahdi-Eddin.*

Visitors' book, May 13, 1851

### The Count of Villeneuve

By the dawn of the nineteenth century Chenonceau had passed into the hands of René Vallet de Villeneuve, who was doubly related to the Dupins: Claude was his grandfather on his mother's side and Madeleine, his great-aunt. Born in Paris in 1777, he had married in 1795, on the morrow of the Terror, Adélaïde Charlotte Apolline de Guibert, the daughter of the famous military strategist, French academician, and correspondent of Julie de Lespinasse, the Count of Guibert, who had died in 1790.

A devoted reader of Guibert's books, Napoleon I wished to help the count's family. He entrusted René Vallet de Villeneuve with several diplomatic missions to Holland, awarded him a count's title, and attached him and his wife to the household of Louis and Hortense Bonaparte, the king and queen of Holland, as first chamberlain and lady of the palace. The events of 1814 obliged the couple to retire to Chenonceau where they lived for the next four decades. This was the Romantic era in France and the winsome, poetic style of the French Renaissance being once again fashionable, the château provided a splendid backdrop for celebrations of the "new" æsthetic. The count and the countess refurbished the interior in the spirit of the sixteenth century.

∧ A Romantic fantasy: Renaissance figures at the foot of the main stairs at Chenonceau. Lithograph by G. Massé, *ca.* 1835.

The lower gallery was decorated with sculpted medallions of historical figures obtained from the administrator of the former Musée des Petits-Champs in Paris.

The gardens too underwent change. A portion of the Parc de Civray was redesigned by Lord Seymour in the English style; exotic trees were planted—cedars, mimosas, sweet gums—as were native plane and locust trees from the park of La Malmaison. A new orangery was built in 1825 on the foundations of the Chapelle Saint-Hubert. Greenhouses and nurseries were added, the main avenue was lined with plane trees, and the entrance of the forecourt was embellished with two stone sphinxes. Renewing the tradition of sericulture at Chenonceau, Madame de Villeneuve had mulberries planted in 1821 and transformed Dupin de Francueil and Jean-Jacques Rousseau's natural history cabinet in Les Dômes into premises for breeding silk worms and spinning silk.[108] In 1853 the owners took steps to have the château officially declared a national historical monument, a richly-deserved classification which meant that it now became a protected site.

Surrounded by their large family, the Villeneuves practiced the very open hospitality of nineteenth-century *châtelains*[109] and received illustrious visitors like the Duke and Duchess of Orléans in 1840 and, in 1851,[110] Abd el-Kader, the emir of Muscara who had opposed the French conquest of Algeria and was detained at the château of Amboise. The beauty of Chenonceau also appealed to writers. Georges Sand, because of her connection with the Dupins, visited the château in 1842. Gustave Flaubert, touring France on foot with his friend Maxime du Camp, wrote in 1847: "I know not what singular sweetness and aristocratic serenity suffuse the château of Chenonceau. It lies some ways from the village, which keeps itself at a respectful distance. You see it at the end of a long tree-lined avenue, surrounded by woods and framed by a vast park with ample lawns. Built on the water, in the air, it lifts up its turrets and square chimneys. The Cher flows beneath it and murmurs at the foot of its arches whose pointed tips break the current. It's peaceful and gentle, elegant and robust. There is nothing boring about its tranquillity, no bitterness

187

[108] Madame de Villeneuve kept a register of the work she undertook at Les Dômes.
[109] Vicomte Joseph Walsch and Alphonse Baillargé, *Album du château de Blois restauré et des châteaux de Chambord, Chenonceaux, Chaumont et Amboise,* Blois: Prévost, 1851, with lithographs after Monthelin's drawings. See also Anatole Chabouillet, *Le Chateau de Chenonceau. Ouvrage pittoresque, architectural et romantique,* lithographs by G. Massé, Paris, n.d. (ca. 1845).
[110] The visitors' book was inaugurated in 1847 with the arrival of the Congrès Scientifique de France.

∧ The new fountain by the architect A. de Saint-Jouan at the center of Diane's parterre, inspired by Du Cerceau's description of the 6-meter tall jet of water spouting from a rock.

∧ Diane's parterre.

One of the sphinxes placed by the Count of Villeneuve where the main avenue joins the forecourt.

∧ Chenonceau and its English-style park in the Romantic era. Lithograph by L. Vairon after a drawing by the Countess of Menou, 1841.

111 G. Flaubert, *Par les champs et par les grèves*, 1885 (published posthumously).
112 Decades earlier, the young Villeneuve had been sent to the Spanish border to inform Napoleon of the birth of his nephew.

in its melancholy."[111] The château's romantic outlines also caught the fancy of two theatrical producers, Sechan and Desplechein, and inspired the settings of Meyerbeer's great success based on a libretto by Eugène Scribe, *Les Huguenots*, when it was performed at the Paris opera in 1836.

The Count of Villeneuve ended his career as senator and honorary chamberlain of Napoleon III.[112] He married off his daughter to the Marquis de la Roche-Aymon, the youngest representative of an eminent royalist family, who retired to Chenonceau and lived in the Pavillon des Marques (in Les Dômes) until his death in 1862. Another resident of the château was the Russian prince Augustin Galitzin, married to Stéphanie de la Roche-Aymon in 1844. He was the first to take an interest in the estate's archives and use them for historical research. This activity placed him in direct competition with the abbé Chevalier, who had been asked to classify the archives scientifically in 1859. A widower since 1852, the Count of Villeneuve died in February 1863, survived by two children, Count Septime de Villeneuve and the Dowager Marquise of La Roche-Aymon. A year and a few weeks later, in April, they sold the château and grounds for 850,000 francs, with the furniture and paintings thrown in for an additional 95,000.

∧ The "César de Vendôme Chamber" on the second floor.

∧ The "Chamber of the Five Queens" on the second floor.

∧ J.-B. Carpeaux, terracotta bust of Marguerite Pelouze, 1872 (Musée de Valenciennes). Modeled when the sculptor was commissioned to design a cenotaph for the Wilson family.

## Marguerite Pelouze

Chenonceau's new owner was a woman. Marguerite-Henriette-Joséphine Wilson was married to Eugène-Philippe Pelouze, the administrator of the Gas Company of Paris and the son of a leading chemist, a disciple of Gay-Lussac and member of the French Academy of Sciences (Théophile-Jules Pelouze, 1807-1867). Eugène Pelouze himself was not one of the château's more memorable masters. His wife, on the other hand, had a powerful personality and, eager to rekindle the memory of the great ladies in whose footsteps she felt fortunate to follow, she made it her mission to restore Chenonceau. Her father, Daniel Wilson, had died in 1849, leaving her and her brother not only an immense fortune but also a taste for the arts and a large collection of paintings.[113] Born in Glasgow in 1789, this Scottish engineer had come to France toward 1810 to work at Le Creusot and later at a steam engine factory at Charenton. Eventually he had set up jointly with the firm of Mauby, an English company supplying gas lighting for the streets of Paris. Eugène Pelouze had been an employee of his.

Having fallen in love with the château, Marguerite decided she wanted to resurrect the romantic beauty of Chenonceau in its heyday, the early French Renaissance. Her brother assisted her in this exciting task. He too was named Daniel Wilson (1840-1919) and served as a deputy for the Indre-et-Loire from 1869 to 1902. With an ardor that matched his sister's, he supervised the work on the château—goaded in his case by a driving ambition to make a name for himself in local politics (both as a deputy and as mayor of the town of Loches),

[113] The collection consisted of paintings accumulated by Baron Massias, the French resident at Karlsruhe, and by the chevalier Bodin-Demolands, who had been in charge of buying art for Joseph Bonaparte.

∧ Carved medallion on the new chapel door.

∧ *The Triumph of Charity*, sixteenth-century
Flanders tapestry in the Bed-chamber
of Diane.

114 The work is described in detail in C. Chevalier's invaluable *Restauration de Chenonceau. 1864-1878*, a copy of which the author wished to present to each of the architects, craftsmen, and workmen who took part in restoring the château.
115 Roguet was born in Dijon. Appointed architect of the City of Paris in 1870, he built the wings overlooking the second court at the Musée Carnavalet after 1871, as well as the annexes of the Hôtel de Ville. Between 1876 and 1878 he built the Archives of the Seine on the Quai Henri IV (recently demolished). He also worked on the churches of L'Isle-Adam and Étampes and on the châteaux of Montrésor and Stors.

local industry, and the arts. For an entire year he and Marguerite researched the château's history, piecing it together from the archives the abbé Chevalier was putting in order. They also made several trips to Italy to study Italian Renaissance designs. Their guiding principle was to respect scrupulously all vestiges of the castle as it had stood in its days of glory and to preserve every authentic fragment of it that could not be left in place.

The restoration work commenced in 1865.[114] During the first three years the builders concentrated on the walls, the openings and the roof. The Pelouze's bankers had authorized a budget of 605,000 francs, but this proved insufficient and, in 1868, new funds were poured into that "colossal undertaking." Altogether the restoration cost 1,500,000 francs, if we are to believe the abbé Chevalier, who seems to have been hugely impressed by this figure. Marguerite Pelouze had placed the ambitious project in the hands of the architect Félix Roguet, who had become famous in 1854 for the construction of the château of Laverdine (near Nérondes, in the department of the Cher). Later he had worked with the Ballu agency on restoring the Tour Saint-Jacques and building the churches of la Trinité and Sainte Clotilde in Paris.[115]

195

∧ The château roofs and the ridge ornaments
Félix Roguet designed for Madame Pelouze.

∧ The wing of Les Dômes restored by Félix Roguet in 1865.

∧ The *Madonna and Child* (fifteenth-century Florentine School) in the chapel loggia.

Roguet's first task in 1865, a kind of trial run, was to remodel Les Dômes, reconstruct its attic in the manner of Philibert de l'Orme, and reorganize the façade by dividing it into harmoniously-spaced bays crowned by dormers. The central pavilion, the roof line of which had been lowered, regained its original volume and was fitted out with pilasters. Louis Borie, a sculptor from Bléré, produced a suitably neo-Renaissance decoration for the building. The interior was converted into lavish stables for Madame Pelouze, with stalls, mangers, and a saddle room built by fashionable carpenters and saddlers.

Next, on May 1, 1866, two masons from Beaulieu named Tertissier and Boizeau set to work on removing Catherine de' Medici's additions to the château. The four herms of the entrance façade were taken down, the original openings of the three bays reconstructed, and a stone balustrade was installed to replace the balcony's iron latticework. The east façade was restored to its initial state by demolishing Queen Louise's chamber and rebuilding the terrace between the chapel and the library, with its original pair of turrets, one of them enclosing a stairway. The décor of the façades, dormers, and chimneys was re-established and completed, a bell was installed over the chapel, and the roof was adorned with a hammered copper crest.

Work began on the interior as well. The flights of the great stone staircase, which had remained unfinished between the first and second stories, were completed and decorated in 1869-1870 in the style of the early Renaissance, complete with medallions depicting Strength, Prudence, and Benevolence carved by the sculptor

Adolphe Geoffroy. Renaissance-style fireplaces were erected in the bed-chambers;
sculpted doors—the chapel doors are particularly splendid—wainscoting, carved
window frames, flagstones and floor tiles imitating surviving elements of the
original décor were lavished on every room. Tall fireplaces were added at either
end of the two galleries. The twin fireplaces in the upper gallery, inspired by the
original south fireplace, were executed in 1874-1876 by Michel Léon Breuil. The
kitchens were equipped with everything needed for entertaining on a grand scale.
Several of the chapel's original stained-glass windows having vanished due to

∧ Stalls in Madame Pelouze's stables in the Dômes.

∧ The kitchen area built inside the piers under the
château. The staff dining quarters.

the alterations undertaken for Catherine de' Medici, three new windows were made
to replace them. Executed by Goguelet after cartoons by Steinheil, they represented
Marguerite Pelouze and her brother as St. Margaret and St. Thomas. Marguerite
even had a crypt built below the chapel to house cenotaphs for her parents
and for herself after she died, and she commissioned the great sculptor Carpeaux,
whom she invited to Chenonceau in 1872, to carve her funeral monument.

∧ The kitchen furnishings installed for Madame
   Pelouze were added to when the château served
   as an army hospital between 1914 and 1918.

> Roasting spits and clockwork drive
   in the kitchen fireplace.

The decoration projects for Chenonceau grew increasingly grandiose. The historian Palustre[116] fretted over a decorative project Madame Pelouze was considering "under the influence of a painter gifted with more facility than talent." This "tawdry Tiepolo" was proposing to imitate the Palazzo Labia frescoes on the gallery walls, with medieval robber barons on one side and the Bohiers landing in Naples on the other. Fortunately, the zeal of this fresco artist from Nantes, named Charles Toché, was stopped in time. The old outside stairs leading from the Marques' Tower to the gardens were torn down and a fifteenth-century *Madonna and Child* Madame Pelouze had bought in Orléans was placed in a niche in the tower.

∧ The four herms from Catherine de' Medici's façade presently located in the Parc de Chisseau.

∧ The new labyrinth designed by Daniel Wilson.

[116] In a text only published in 1895.

It was chiefly in the gardens that Marguerite's brother, Daniel Wilson, exercised his energy. In 1867 he began reconstructing the alleys, terraces, and parterres sacrificed to the Villeneuve's taste for English gardens. He designed a new labyrinth for the Parc de Chisseau and had it laid out behind Catherine de' Medici's herms, between which a *cabinet,* or green room, was built. He reorganized Diane's parterre, from which he had an immense ilex dating from Catherine's time removed. The paths were made to meet at 90° and 45° angles at the central fountain, delimiting triangular beds decorated with floral embroideries against a background of colored sand. This design was based on the Italian manner inspired, or so  the abbé Chevalier believed, by the Roman gardens of the Villa Pamphili and the Villa Albani. There were plans to set up a marble group in the center, representing the birth of Venus, to be carved by the voguish sculptor Carrier-Belleuse. Catherine's new parterre was to be graced likewise with the addition of "a woman caught by a sudden shower who takes refuge in the shelter of a grotesque faun" commissioned from Léon Breuil. Neither of these two groups was actually installed.

Venice was in fashion then on the banks of the Cher. Marguerite Pelouze gave sumptuous parties at Chenonceau. One in particular was memorable: organized by the painter Toché, the "tawdry Tiepolo," it featured gondolas on the river clustering around a reconstruction of a doge's galley. The guest of honor was no less than the President of the Republic, Jules Grevy (whose daughter, Alice, Daniel Wilson had married in 1881). The "Grand Canal" atmosphere of the occasion is evoked skillfully on a tapestry woven at Neuilly in 1883 after a cartoon by Walmez and recently acquired by the château.

But the delightful breezes of Chenonceau soon turned into icy blasts. The urbane Daniel Wilson, who had been one of President Grévy's early republican supporters, revealed himself to be a glib, mindless, less-than-honest politician. Appointed under-secretary of state of finances in 1879, he took advantage of his position to launch newspapers favorable to his politics, *La Petite France du Centre et de l'Ouest* and, especially, *Le Moniteur de l'Exposition universelle* which sought to attract subscribers by giving them hope that their support would

[114] Cf. G.Vapereau, *Dictionnaire universel des contemporains*, Paris, 1893.

∧ Chenonceau, Venetian-style. The tapestry woven at Neuilly
in 1883 after a cartoon by Walmez hangs in the third-floor
gallery-corridor.

gain them the ribbon of the Legion of Honor.[117] The affair broke in 1887. Hit hard by the scandal, President Grévy, an extremely punctilious republican, very proud of his re-election in 1885, immediately handed in his resignation.

"Ah, what a misfortune it is to have a son-in-law!" hummed the crowds in Paris. Meanwhile the banks began to panic over the huge sums squandered at Chenonceau and, in 1889, the Crédit foncier got a court order to have the estate auctioned.

## The Meniers

In 1891 Chenonceau was thus sold to Emilio Terry,[118] a wealthy American who lived in Cuba. Twenty-two years later Terry sold it to Henri Menier, the scion of a celebrated dynasty of chocolate manufacturers. Henri's grandfather, Jean-Antoine Brutus, a Tourangeau peasant who had "gone up" to Paris to become a druggist, and his father, Émile-Justin, had founded the family business, which had quickly grown into the world's leading chocolate manufacturer. Weakened and in poor health, Émile had handed over the firm in 1881 to his three sons, Henri, Gaston, and Albert. What reason, one wonders, did Henri have for acquiring Chenonceau if not the mysterious affinity between the site of the Bohiers' château and that of the Menier's head office in a mill on an arm of the Marne at Noisiel (the river drove the chocolate-making machinery and provided convenient transportation)? The coincidence seems too great to be altogether fortuitous.[119]

[117] See G. Vapereau, *Dictionnaire universel des contemporains,* Paris, 1893.

[118] Emilio Terry also bought roughly 100 valuable paintings, including a Corregio, a Ribera, and the château's famous Diane. However, the château's collection of small sixteenth-century portraits was broken up and dispersed among different buyers. Emilio Terry is the father of the well-known interior decorator.

[119] The very handsome polychrome building erected in 1867 by the architect Jules Saulnier still exists and now houses Nestlé France. See *Nestlé France à Noiseuil,* Paris, 1996.

Henri died the year he purchased the château. He left it to his brother Gaston, who then not only took charge of the family business but entered politics as well, serving successively as mayor, *conseiller général,* deputy, and senator of the Seine-et-Marne. When World War I broke out a year later, Gaston Menier decided to contribute to the national effort by setting up a temporary hospital at Chenonceau. One hundred and twenty beds were placed in the two galleries over the Cher. All expenses were paid by Gaston until, with the return of peace, the hospital was disbanded on December 31, 1918.[120] Gaston's daughter-in-law, Madame Georges Menier, a registered hospital matron, actively assisted the physicians and surgeons, and 2,254 wounded soldiers were cared for during the four war years.

[120] See the anonymous brochure *Le Château de Chenonceau,* Paris: G. Cadet, June 1921.

207

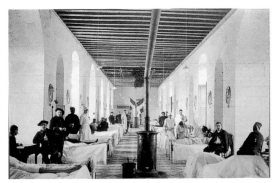

∧ The lower gallery transformed into a 50-bed hospital ward during World War I.

∧ Nurses in front of the upper gallery "fireplace of the captives."

Chenonceau still belongs to the Menier family. Every Menier generation, that of Gaston, Georges, Hubert, and now Pauline and Jean-Louis Menier, and Jean-Louis' wife Laure, has set its heart on maintaining and enriching that national treasure to the best of its abilities, and on making it more widely known.

∧ Madame Georges Menier as a hospital matron.

ICI FURENT SOIGNES
2254 BLESSES
PENDANT ʟᴀ GUERRE
1914 – 1918

∧ Plaque to the wounded who were cared for
at Chenonceau.

[121] M. Yourcenar, *Sous bénéfice d'inventaire*, a collection of essays which includes an evocation of Chenonceau entitled "Ah! mon beau château" (Ah, my lovely castle), Paris: Gallimard, 1978, pp. 56-115.

Among the challenges the Meniers have had to face, the Cher flooded in May 1940, causing significant damage, and in 1944 the chapel's stained-glass windows were shattered by bombing (Max Ingrand was commissioned to replace them in 1954). The sheer scale of the almost 400-acre (160-hectare) estate and its vineyards, which occupy one-third of the domain, required permanent full-time management. Appointed in 1951, Bernard Voisin was placed in charge of curating the château and its collections and opening them to a steady stream of, by now, over 800,000 visitors a year.

Respect for the château's history and the need for providing clear information have dictated the latest restoration of Chenonceau's interior. The galleries, across which many clandestine travelers escaped between 1940 and 1942 over the line of demarcation between German-held northern France and the Free Zone, now house temporary exhibitions of contemporary art. A wax museum was set up in Madame Pelouze's former stables in Les Dômes. The museum's theme, the "Gallery of Ladies," pays tribute to all the women who shaped Chenonceau's buildings and gardens, all those who exclaimed, as does the voice of posterity in an essay by Marguerite Yourcenar:[121] *"Ah! mon beau château."*

Names of persons in capital letters, names of places in lower case.

212

ANDROUET DU CERCEAU, Jacques, *Les Plus Excellents Bastiments de France*, Paris, 2 vols., 1576 and 1579. Reprinted with comments by David Thomson, Paris: Sand Conti, 1988.

*Architecture, jardin, paysage. L'environnement du château et de la villa aux XVe et XVIe siècles,* papers of a colloquium held in Tours in 1992, Paris: Picard, 1999 ("De Architectura").

AUBERT, Marcel, "Château de Chenonceaux," *Congrès archéologique de la France*. Tours, 1948, Paris, 1949, pp. 226-230.

BABELON, Jean-Pierre, *Châteaux de France au siècle de la Renaissance,* Paris: Flammarion-Picard, 1989.

BLUNT, Anthony, *Philibert de l'Orme,* London: Zwemmer, 1958.

CHATENET (Monique), *La Cour de France au XVIe siècle. Vie sociale et architecture*, Paris: Picard, 2002 ("De Architectura").

CHEVALIER, abbé Casimir, *Archives royales de Chenonceau*, vol. I, *Pièces historiques relatives à la châtellenie*, Paris: Téchener, 1864; vol. II, *Comptes de receptes et despences faites par Diane de Poitiers,* Paris: Téchener, 1864; vol. III, *Lettres et devis de Philibert de l'Orme,* Paris: Téchener, 1864; vol. IV, *Debtes et créanciers de la Royne mère Catherine de Médicis,* Paris: Téchener, 1862; vol. V, *Diane de Poitiers au Conseil du Roi,* Paris: Aubry, 1866. Historical introduction in the beginning of vol. I, table of the first three vols. at the back of vol. III.

CHEVALIER, abbé Casimir, *La vigne, les jardins et les vers à soie à Chenonceau au XVIe siècle,* Tours: Ladevèze, 1860.

CHEVALIER, abbé Casimir, *Les Jardins de Catherine de Médicis à Chenonceau. 1563-1565,* Tours: Ladevèze, 1868.

CHEVALIER, abbé Casimir, *Restauration de Chenonceau. 1864-1878,* Lyon: Perrin et Martinet, 1878.

CHEVALIER, abbé Casimir, *Histoire de Chenonceau, ses artistes, ses fêtes, ses vicissitudes,* Lyon: Perrin, 1868.

CHEVALIER, abbé Casimir, *Le château de Chenonceau, notice historique,* Tours: Mazereau, 1869 (third edition), Bousrey, 1882 (fifth edition).

CHEVALIER, abbé Casimir, *Histoire abrégée de Chenonceau,* Lyon: Perrin et Martinet, 1879.

CLOULAS, Ivan, *Catherine de Médicis,* Paris: Fayard, 1979.

CLOULAS, Ivan, *La Vie quotidienne dans les châteaux de la Loire au temps de la Renaissance,* Paris: Hachette, 1983.

CLOULAS, Ivan, *Diane de Poitiers,* Paris: Fayard, 1997.

GEBELIN, François, *Les Châteaux de la Renaissance,* Paris: Les Beaux-Arts, 1927, pp. 81-86.

GEBELIN, François, *Les Châteaux de la Loire,* Paris: Alpina, 1957, pp. 65-68.

GUILLAUME, Jean, "Chenonceaux avant la construction de la galerie. Le château de Thomas Bohier et sa place dans l'architecture de la Renaissance," *Gazette des Beaux-Arts*, January 1969, pp. 19-46.

GUILLAUME, Jean, "Un joyau de pierre," in *Chenonceau,* special issue of *Connaissance des arts*, 2001, pp. 28-43. This issue, which is prefaced by Alain Decaux, also contains articles by Bernard Voisin ("Renaissance"), Axelle de Gaineron ("Les dames de Chenonceau"), Didier Moulin ("La galerie des Dames"), and Ivan Cloulas ("Un théâtre de verdure").

NORMAND, Jean-Paul, *Le Château de Chenonceau,* Chambray-lès-Tours, 1973 (anthology).

PALUSTRE, Léon, article on Chenonceau in HAVARD, H., *La France artistique et monumentale,* vol. VI, Paris, 1895, pp. 169-192.

PÉROUSE DE MONTCLOS, Jean-Marie, *Philibert De l'Orme, architecte du roi (1514-1570),* Paris: Mengès, 2000.

RANJARD, Dr. Robert, *Le Château de Chenonceau,* Paris & Tours, 1950.

TERRASSE, Charles, *Le Château de Chenonceau,* Paris: Laurens ("Petites Monographies"), 1928.

WEIGERT, Roger-Armand, *Chenonceau,* Paris: Vincent et Fréal ("Les Plus Excellents Bâtiments de France"), 1970.

WOODBRIDGE, Kenneth, *Princely Gardens. The Origins and Development of the French Formal Style*, London: Thames & Hudson, 1986.

215

Photographic credits

All the photographs in this book are by
Jean-Pierre Godeaut except:

Archives photographiques, Coll. Médiathèque
  du Patrimoine, © CMN, Paris: p. 22, 52.
BNF, Paris: p. 28, 45, 93.
Bridgeman-Giraudon-Lauros: p. 96.
Photoflash: cover, pp. 138-139.
RMN/Hervé Lewandowski: p. 62. RMN: p. 125.
  RMN/R.G. Ojeda: p. 194.
Scala: p. 100.
The British Museum: p. 80, 104, 109 (2).

Printed by EuroGrafica S.p.A., Vicenza, Italy, June 2002.